MEMOIRS OF MAYHEM

The Good, The Bad, and The Hilarious

Amber Christensen

Cover Design by Anne Zimanski
Interior Design by Lorie DeWorken, MIND*the*MARGINS, LLC

ISBN-13: 978-0-692-44125-1

Published in the United States

To all the regular people,

doing all the regular things.

To Nick,

who is anything but regular.

And to my friend Mary,

who taught me laughter is the best medicine.

TABLE OF CONTENTS

BUCKLE UP AND HOLD ON TIGHT

Eight-year-old Jackson was repeatedly kicking his soccer ball at the front door because it was too cold to play outside, the constant banging of which resonated throughout the house. Blake, the six-year-old, was growling at his four-year-old brother Aaron, who was breathing down his neck trying to watch him play the Nintendo DS. Aaron wanted me to play catch with him and his new blue mitt for the seventeenth time, but I was too busy discovering a pain worse than stepping on a Lego as eleven-month-old Alex wrapped his tiny fingers around a lock of my long brown hair and used it to pull himself up. *Um, ouch!* I needed a breather, so I left the chaos to my husband Nick and went for a drive in the dismal December darkness.

I drove around and thought about how I used to be so good at life. I graduated from college, lived in Europe, and once held a well-paying job. I also had lofty ambitions for what my children would be like: perfect. It couldn't possibly be that hard to raise quiet, polite, hard-working, respectful, organized, clean, and loving geniuses. The most entertaining part about my parenting ideals was that before my first little bundle of boy entered the world, I actually believed them. In the beginning things went well; then we brought him home from the hospital.

Parenthood makes me feel like I know absolutely nothing about anything and rubs that fact in my face daily. I love my kids, but the incessant noise and craziness a house full of boys inherently creates can darn near do me in. I raise my voice too frequently, hide the Candyland cards that send our gingerbread men back to the bottom of the board so the game will end faster, and blissfully ignore my kids when they hit the play button again after their Mickey Mouse movie ends. What's wrong with letting them watch it over and over as long as they're learning colors and numbers? My ideals have gone from perfection to, "It's okay if you're wearing two different shoes and only one sock. Just get in the car!"

I once heard a story about a little boy who wakes up on his mom's birthday and decides to make her a chocolate cake. He sets a bowl on the counter then fills a cup full of flour, dusting the floor with white powder as he carries it across the kitchen, and dumps it in the bowl. Next, he adds some cocoa and vegetable oil, a cold cube of butter, and a hefty helping of sugar. The boy climbs onto the counter to mix his concoction and stirs as fast as he can. As he stirs with all his might, flinging batter everywhere, his dad appears. The boy follows his dad's eyes around the room, from the flour on the floor to the batter all over the counter to his cocoa-stained face, and realizes in his attempt to make something good he has created a disaster.

Motherhood, despite my good intentions, often leaves me feeling like I'm making a huge mess. Yet, I'm supposed to be the one restoring order. My shortcomings bulldoze my confidence, and I don't always like the person I am at the end of the day. Sometimes I wonder how my husband still loves the mess I see in the mirror. My family deserves someone who patiently gives them her all, not someone who steals the good candy out of their Halloween buckets after they go to bed then shamelessly goes back for seconds.

But we are good at Friday night pizza parties that end with everyone watching a movie from the inside of a blanket fort. We also take the kids to shoot hoops and go swimming at the city rec center fairly often, so at least we're promoting an active lifestyle. Last but nowhere near least, the three kids I've potty trained are all still alive (even though the first round took an entire year). Three down, one to go.

If there is one absolute truth about parenting, it's that it is full of ups, downs, and a lot of in-betweens. So buckle up, hold on tight, and prepare for a roller coaster ride through the good, the bad, and the hilarious.

WHAT'S YOUR NAME KID?

I can be looking right at one of my kids and still call them by the wrong name. I say their names so often, my brain has apparently turned them into a single word: *Jacksonblakeaaronalex*. We chose the name "Alex" because it has special meaning to me, but giving names that both start with "A" to the two youngest may not have been wise. Sometimes, after I've said a few different names (even if the correct one was in there somewhere), I'll look at the child I'm talking to and ask, "What's your name kid?" They think it's funny, but I'm not kidding! To help tell them apart, here's a nutshell rundown of the troops who occupy my house.

Jackson is the oldest. He has a quick mind, and if his brain or body isn't doing something, he gets bored in a hurry. Jackson is obsessed with all things soccer: playing soccer, watching soccer, and reading about professional soccer players. He also keeps a ball in the car to make sure he's never without one. His need to constantly be engaged in activity, which is almost always soccer related, has earned him the name "Action Jackson."

Second is "Birthday Cake Blake." Blake turns every situation into a party and will invite anyone willing to break out in song or show off their dance moves to join him. He loves to tell jokes, make up silly words, and laugh at himself. Life is his party, and if people get in his way, he'll cry if he wants to.

Aaron is number three. Most words that rhyme with his name describe him well. "Blarin' Aaron" is by far the loudest person in our house, and I dare say he is also one of the loudest kids west of the Mississippi. "Darin' Aaron" illustrates his adventurous spirit; he is always up for trying something new. "Scarin' Aaron" also fits him well, and sums up two of his personality traits. He likes to hide, then jump out and roar at people as they walk by; even strangers. We never know what he is going to do or say next, which can also be scary.

Finally, there's "Baby Alex." When he is receiving his high school diploma, he'll still be Baby Alex to us. He is a charmer through and through and has a huge, slobbery grin that's usually concealed by a binky. We call it his secret smile, but it's not a very big secret, because he shares it with everybody.

GROCERY STORE 3 ADVENTURES

There's nothing like a brand new, half-broken bag of pretzels courtesy of Aaron sitting on them in the cart. He also learned if you pick up the red "Guest Services" phone at Target, someone will say hello to you. Where were you on that one Mom? Oh yeah, untangling Blake from a Hula Hoop. Why, oh why, do I ever think taking all my kids to the store will be any less of an adventure than it has always been?

———

One of the biggest bites of reality parenthood shoved into my mouth was that taking kids to the grocery store is no small feat. When I was new to the two-year-old-and-a-baby combo, a typical trip to the store began with me setting Blake's car seat in the bed of the cart while Jackson tried to run away as fast as he could to avoid capture. When I caught him and tried to lift him into the seat, he immediately started kicking and flailing about. I promised him the entire universe if he would sit down and let me buckle him in without waging a world war, but trying to reason with a toddler is as useless as a CapriSun without a straw.

A trip to the store would not be complete without judging looks from others, which simultaneously say, "You are the worst mother on planet earth," and, "How dare you bring that kid out in public?" Believe me folks, I would rather not. No bunch of bananas, carton of milk, or chocolate donut for that matter is worth the drama. But leaving my rambunctious entourage at home isn't always feasible, especially when my husband is out of town and we need medicine, or diapers; or to get the heck out of the house.

When Nick is gone on business, relief from the decibels and demands of the little ones doesn't come until bedtime, and staying home together all day long can seem like the worst idea ever. So I occasionally risk a trip to the grocery store in order to have a change of scenery. When I'm on my own, the kids instinctively know I'm in survival mode and ask for things I don't usually buy. I play right into their hands and load up on frozen pizza, Swedish Fish, and Cinnamon Toast Crunch. We almost make it through a whole shopping experience without causing a scene, until we stop to get a movie from the Redbox kiosk on the way out. Aaron comes apart when I tell him we're not getting a movie we've already rented so many times we could have bought it, and everyone who passes the mom that won't rent her hysterical child a $1.50

DVD stares me down. *Who was I kidding?* Taking all the kids to the store holds its place as the worst idea ever.

From the ages of one to three, Blarin' Aaron brought on disapproving looks and unsolicited advice from strangers in every store in town. In one of his most vocal displays of discontent, he was screaming so loudly while trying to free himself from the grocery cart seat belt that a woman followed us to investigate. I knew she was behind us, but kept filling my cart with school lunch what-nots as if she wasn't there.

The Silent Speech Giver in my head, who occasionally escapes even though I try not to let her out, wanted me to turn around and say, "I dare you to give it a shot lady. Come see if you can calm him down. I'll give you five minutes but you'll be begging for mercy in two."

When the woman realized I wasn't torturing Aaron, she came up to me and said, "Wow, I thought he was being hurt, but he really just wants to get out, doesn't he?" I was amazed that she dared to tell me she thought I was hurting my child in the middle of a grocery store, but I kept the Silent Speech Giver at bay.

"Yes, he would much rather run around but I'll never be able to catch him," was all I said.

Another time, I was cleaning my house for overnight guests and ran out of toilet bowl cleaner. I needed some ASAP, so I loaded Aaron into the car and headed to the store without showering, wearing dirty sweatpants and an old T-shirt. I'm sure everyone who saw me that day felt sorry for the guy who married me, but true ugliness is a virtue; many are called, but few are chosen.

On the way to the checkout counter, Aaron threw a tantrum over the Peanut M&M's I wasn't about to buy. I was happy to spring for the regular variety, but those are no fun since he can't suck the chocolate off of the peanuts and spit them on the floor. A woman strolled by with her cart and shot me the look of death. I did look a lot like Medusa, so maybe she was frozen in her tracks. Right then I came up with a way to answer that look, and every variation of it I'd been given over the years, without saying a word. Aaron needed a custom-made baseball cap that said, "Would you want to stay home with me all day?"

Some stores provide car-carts with toy steering wheels in them to make grocery shopping more enjoyable for kids. Our car-cart store has exactly two, so if we're lucky enough to see one, we race to snag it. While it does provide some entertainment, what's even more entertaining is me trying to push the monstrous thing. Once when I pushed a car-cart over a tiny bump, Aaron hit his mouth on the plastic steering wheel. He cried loud enough to wake Baby Alex, who joined in on the cry-fest from his car seat. Competing to be heard over all the crying, six-year-old Blake screamed, "Crying expert! Crying expert! We have a crying expert!" I might as well have walked into the store and shouted, "We're he-ere!"

In addition to dirty looks and meltdowns, shopping trips can also offer unexpected opportunities to teach kids about honesty. When Jackson needed new soccer shorts, he picked some out and hung them on the side of the cart while we finished shopping. We got to the checkout counter, where the cashier was a chatterbox, and within seconds Aaron had run off to the drinking fountain. In the midst of listening to the cashier talk, trying to keep an eye on Aaron, and putting the rest of our items on the counter, I forgot all about the soccer shorts hanging hidden behind the baby's car seat.

It wasn't until the kids were piling into the car that I noticed the shorts were still there. I checked my receipt, hoping by some saving grace the cashier had scanned the tag and left the shorts where they were. No such luck. I sighed and told the kids to unbuckle so we could go back in and pay for the shorts. Jackson was surprisingly excited. "Mom! I've heard stories about this at church!" he said. I wasn't happy that I had to haul the kids back into the store, but it was worth it to bring the lesson to life.

Unfortunately, my grocery store embarrassments also stretch into times when I go shopping alone. The very day I was talking with friends about how much dumber I got after having kids, I found myself in the produce section with my shirt on inside out. *Seriously?!*

One night, for the well-being of everyone under our roof, Nick sent me away for some alone time. I headed to the store that sells chocolate in bulk. As I was walking down the cereal aisle contemplating whether to pay full price for my favorite kind or wait until it went on sale, my sister called. I mindlessly pushed my cart forward and told her about my Chocolate Chex dilemma. I started to turn the corner and *WHAM!* I rammed right into a display of gummy bears. No less than fifteen five-pound bags went crashing to the ground. I told my sister I would call her back and closed my flip phone, accidentally dropping it. It hit the floor as well, and the battery went spinning three feet away. A young couple watched the spectacle unfold, but pretended not to notice and kept walking. Maybe I need a, "Would you want to stay home with me all day?" baseball cap for myself. I reassembled my phone and re-stacked the gummy bears, wondering why there are no warnings about the dangers of talking on the phone while shopping.

My favorite trip to the store was just before Mother's Day when I saw a frustrated dad and his four little kids trying to find their wife and mother a gift. After repeatedly asking one of the children not to climb on the shelf and losing another, the dad said, "Come on guys. Why does it have to be such a big deal just to go to the store?" That realization is the best present he could have found.

MILES OF PILES

Me, in the car: Now we get to go home and do my favorite thing—fold laundry!

Jackson, not picking up on the sarcasm: I thought your favorite thing was going to Costco.

I told him what my real favorite thing to do is and he was surprised. Maybe one day my kids will realize moms are actually people.

———

As sure as the sun rises each morning, there will always be laundry to do. Life in the mommy lane is littered with it: a sock here, a pair of pajamas there, and mountains of sheets and towels to wash everywhere. Laundry is always there, doing what it does best, which is never go away.

Laundry should be spelled "lawn-dry." As in, pull the

clothes out of the washer and throw them out on the lawn so the sun can do the rest. When the clothes are dry, the kids can collect the ones that are theirs and put them away. Or, throw them on the ground in front of their dresser, which is where Aaron's clean clothes usually hang out. When he chooses what to wear, instead of pushing the ones he doesn't want to the other side of the drawer, he throws them on the ground until he finds something he likes. The pile of clean clothes often ends up in his hamper, adding an annoying step to the laundry sorting process. While separating lights and darks, I also have to pull out the clean clothes and put them back where they belong. If it wasn't socially unacceptable to look like your mom doesn't care about you, I would throw them back on the floor because that's where they'll end up the next time he gets dressed anyway.

Other than a white flag for mom to wave when an especially hectic night calls for ordering pizza and surrendering to the call of a hot bath, homes with little ones shouldn't contain much of anything white. White shirts on children confess everything they put into their mouths, becoming napkins for orange Cheeto hands, ketchup spilled out the bottom of hot dog buns, and the incriminating chocolate slobber created by treats sneaked from mom's (not so) secret stash.

If mom wears a white shirt, it becomes a tissue for the tear-stained, runny-nosed face of the child whose ice cream toppled off its cone and bounced from the shirt to the pavement. It also makes a great spit rag for the baby who turns his head just before he burps, missing the burp cloth on mom's shoulder altogether. There's nothing like the warm feeling that comes from regurgitated milk. A useful baby shower gift that would offer endless possibilities for instantaneous disaster cleanup would be a mom bib made from an over-sized beach towel that would cover her down to the knee.

In the 1960s, paper clothing became a popular fashion trend. It fizzled out fairly quickly, but the idea of wearing a dress a few times then throwing it away does sound appealing: no folding, ironing, or dry cleaning. My motivation to switch the laundry comes more from knowing clothes taken out of the dryer the moment it buzzes don't have to be ironed than it does from wanting clean clothes. It also comes from knowing if my favorite jeans are dirty, nothing says get to the gym like a pair I haven't worn for a while. Or a pair that shrinks a size when my kids husband accidentally runs it through the dryer (but bless his soul for trying!).

If your well-meaning significant other dries your jeans, dryer stretches can help minimize the damage. Put one leg into your shrunken jeans and pull until you can't pull them up any higher. Then put the other leg in and pull with all your might. You may have to jump up and down a few times; it doesn't make your jeans fit any better, but it will make you think they do. When it seems like your pants couldn't be any more uncomfortable, they will finally button. Combine lunges with squats to stretch your jeans out as much as possible. Do this each time you put them on until you're not sure if your jeans are stretching or your body is shrinking. Either way, as long you can breathe when the pants are both buttoned and zipped, you win!

I'm convinced the ever-baffling question of whether washers eat socks is a huge cover up for moms who refuse to stick their hand inside a wet, stinky, balled-up sports sock. Those sweat-soaked socks may not bite, but they sure leave a repulsive aftertaste. Instead of risking their health, maybe some moms simply pick them up with the tips of their fingernails and drop them into the garbage can.

Nobody likes to wash nasty socks, but it's all in the name of love, right? Wrong. I was sitting on the sidelines at soccer practice discussing sweaty socks with other moms and told them I washed my sons' soccer socks once in a ball to get rid of the smell, then pulled them flat and washed them again so they wouldn't be crusty. Creating expectations like that put the other moms to shame, and I was told to stop immediately. They didn't have to tell me twice! I now wash sports socks only once, the same way they end up in the middle of the floor, whether they are balled-up, inside out, or tied together.

Even more perplexing than the sock-eating washer mystery is laundry's ability to multiply exponentially. I could wash, dry, and fold clothes all day every day and the hampers would keep spitting out more. Just as well that I don't, because on the rare occasion when all the laundry is done for all of about seven minutes, there are never enough hangers. And that necessitates a trip to the grocery store, which should be avoided at all costs.

WEAR A HAZMAT SUIT

Blake: When Dad gets home, he'll say, 'Who let our house look like this?' And I'll say,' It was a bear.' Three little bears indeed.

———

Blake came to me making a sound that was a mix between a cry and a whine. A *chrine*, if you will. "Mom, I bit my tongue," he chrined.

"Sorry dude, but I'm not going to kiss it better," I said with a smile.

"Yuck Mom!" he replied, now laughing. "Hey Mom, sometimes if I have something on my tongue I lick the carpet to get it off." I thought of everything that has ever walked on, been spilled on, or been dragged across the carpet and wished I could have died in my ignorance. All I have to say for my carpet is at least the ketchup that got spilled on it matches the smashed strawberries and red crayon that were already there. Yuck Blake!

The most useful cleaning tip I've found is one I happened upon accidentally. When we had spaghetti for dinner, my eighteen-month-old threw as much on the floor as he put in his mouth. He ended up with tomato sauce on his face and tummy, and in his hair and belly button. I bathed him and put him to bed but conveniently forgot to clean up the messy kitchen. The next morning, the dried out noodles under the high chair were a cinch to sweep up. That beats trying to wipe up rolling, squishy noodles any day.

No matter how many quotes I read justifying a messy house, like, "Our house was clean last week, sorry you missed it," or, "Sorry about the mess, but we live here," the only thing that really makes me feel better is seeing other houses in the same state of disarray. I get a sick and twisted sense of relief when I notice someone else's trash can lid as sticky and yogurt-spattered as mine. The only mommy competition I could win would be for leaving exploded chili beans on the roof of the microwave the longest. Actually, I could also win for having the most containers full of leftovers we'll never eat sitting in the fridge, right next to the molding good intentions I had when I bought organic snap peas.

Not everyone shares my excitement about other people's housekeeping flaws. I babysat a three-year-old neighbor boy and when his mom picked him up, she took him into the bathroom. When they came out, she said, "You know what I do sometimes if I don't have time to clean my bathroom?"—Slap to the face.—"I just get those sanitizing wipes and do a quick wipe down so it looks clean even if I didn't scrub it." A few days later I watched her son again, and again she took him to the bathroom. I still hadn't touched it. There's one way to guarantee you'll never get asked to watch someone else's kid again.

My three rules for cleaning the kids' bathroom are: wear a hazmat suit, flush the toilet before looking inside, and do not ask questions. I can clean the bathroom to the point that the porcelain is sparkling and after one kid uses it, there is a hand towel on the floor, water everywhere, and the toilet is colors it shouldn't be. I have wiped off the countertop and had the rag turn yellow. *Really guys, on the counter?*

Before school one morning, I walked past the bathroom door just as one of my boys was coming out. The light was off but I didn't hear a flush, so I asked him to take care of it. "Well I couldn't flush the toilet because it was too dark to see the handle," he said. When I realized he never turned the light on in the first place, it clicked: every time I heard the bathroom door close in the middle of the night, the situation was probably the same. *Seriously kid, if you can't see well enough to flush the toilet, don't use it at all. Just turn on the light!*

I've also had a child pee straight into the garbage can. If his aim is that good, I need to paint a target inside the toilet so he'll aim into the bowl. My friend Becky is a housekeeping magician. She has four little kids yet manages to keep her house spic 'n span. Even the bathroom perpetually smells like lemon. I finally asked Becky how she keeps her bathroom so clean with boys using it. "If I know people are coming over, I clean it and tape it off so nobody can use it until they leave," she said. Genius!

I teach my kids to load the dishwasher, throw clothes from the washer into the dryer, and sweep the floor when they're young enough to think it's fun. It's the perfect trap; once they realize it's work, they can't claim they don't know how to do it. However, teaching a two-year-old to do chores means Wii controllers end up in the dishwasher and shoes end up in the trash can (probably next to my prescription eyeglasses, which mysteriously disappeared after he helped pick up).

Some chores my kids aren't allowed to help with, like cleaning out the toy room. Cleaning up the toy room, yes. Cleaning *out* the toy room, not so much. I once tried to foster benevolence in them by having each kid choose some toys to give away. They emerged from the toy room carrying the toys they selected in the bottoms of their shirts and dumped them on the table for inspection. Their sacrifices consisted of plastic green army men, random dominoes, stray Uno cards, and a few Hot Wheels cars. The entire collection could have fit into a sandwich bag.

I got a box for toys we were going to give away and went in to help them. Everything I threw in the box came right back out to be played with for the first time in months. "Oh Mom, we have to keep this, it's my favorite," I heard. There was also plenty of, "I've been looking for this!" They hadn't looked very hard, because the rediscovered toys were right where the kids left them: in the black hole that is the toy box.

The next day while Jackson was at school and Aaron was taking a nap, I completed the project on my own. Blake was coloring at the table and seemed oblivious to what I was doing, so I worked quickly hoping he wouldn't get bored and come join me for round two of, "Don't you dare throw my broken toys away."

When Jackson got home, he noticed the toy room was unusually clean. "Wow Mom, you cleaned the toy room all by yourself!" he said.

Blake responded before I could. "She took some of our toys away."

Jackson's eyes got big. "She really did?"

"Yeah, they're in the garage. I saw her."

So much for the oblivious preschooler I thought I was fooling, the little sell-out! Jackson wanted to see the toys I boxed up in case he needed to rescue a few, but I put off letting him and he soon forgot about them. A few weeks later, I dropped them off at a donation center. Not once did the kids ask for something I got rid of, or notice anything specific was missing. I wonder if that would work for the old high school T-shirts my husband still has, pit stains and all.

AFTER SCHOOL CIRCUS

Blake: Is there corn in my corn dog?

Me: No.

Blake: Then why is it called that?

Me: I don't know, it just is.

Blake: I'll probably ask Jackson when he gets home from school.

———

The first hour after school gets out is a circus. It begins in the parking lot with that one person who ignores the "Exit Only" sign and enters in the wrong way. They react to honking horns and hands being thrown into the air as if they don't understand the problem. This causes a break in the line of bumper-to-bumper rule followers and throws off the entire space-time continuum of the pick-up process.

The Silent Speech Giver has plenty to say in this situation. *The entrance is only a two second drive from the exit people! See how you're the only car facing the other direction? It's spring and we've been doing this all year; if you still haven't figured it out, you should probably be inside the school.*

Add to the confusion the clown who decides to put their car in park while they run into the school "real quick," and top it off with the acrobatic moves of those trying to back out of actual parking spaces into the pick-up line and we could charge admission to our circus; all we're missing is a big top and a tight rope.

The poor teacher doubling as a crossing guard is no match for carpool anarchy. To combat the chaos, the school needs to hire a member of the TSA to blow their whistle and shout orders. "Keep moving! No parking! Unattended backpacks will be confiscated! Keep moving!"

Once we escape the melee, my kids tell me what they learned that day, including things their friends have that they don't. Here are a few of my favorite examples:

Jackson: One of my friends gave me a super yummy treat today at lunch but I don't know what it's called.

Me: What was it like?

Jackson: It had chocolate around it and a white line of frosting on top.

Me: Was it a chocolate cupcake with white cream in the middle?

Jackson: Yeah.

Me: Those are yummy. They're called Hostess CupCakes.

Jackson: Well first Hayden ate the cream out of the middle. Then he gave it to Brandon. Then Brandon gave it to me.

Well that changes things. Here's a hint my little man: If one of your friends passes on a "super yummy treat," you shouldn't eat it either.

———

Blake: Mom, some kids in kindergarten have their own phones.

Jackson: Yeah, some kids in my class do too.

Blake: When will we?

Me, deciding on the spot: Not until you're eighteen.

Blake: Well, at least we have wallets.

At least.

Sometimes on the drive home, my kids have me questioning whether I deserve my college degree. When Jackson learned about cell anatomy in second grade, he told me all about lysosomes and ribosomes. Then he asked, "Mom, do you know what ER is short for?" Emergency Room is the only ER I'm familiar with. In relation to biology, I had nothing. The cell, the most basic form of all living things, and I couldn't even remember enough about it to impress an eight-year-old.

"I don't remember," I finally admitted.

"Endoplasmic Reticulum," Jackson said. Then he tested me again, "Do you know any other parts of the cell Mom?" I could picture the cell diagram from my old textbooks that looks like a fried egg, but couldn't recall what any of the labels on it said.

"Nucleus!" I finally answered, way too enthusiastically. Then I changed the subject and reminded the kids they needed to feed the bunny when we got home to save myself from any additional cell-related questions.

Once inside the house, Act II of the circus begins. Each child thinks they're the ring master and starts rattling off demands. "Mom, I need a pencil for my homework, and can you get me a drink? Also we need to go buy some index cards tonight," Jackson says. Blake also wants to be heard that instant, so he talks over his brother. "I need a snack. I'm so, so hungry," he says, followed by, "Oh yeah Mom, I need to take a treat to school tomorrow for my birthday because they're celebrating all the kids who have summer birthdays at the same time."

System overload!

One especially crazy afternoon, Alex screamed all the way home from picking up the older boys, impatiently waiting to be fed. As soon as we walked in the house, I sat on the couch to nurse him. Jackson sat on a stool at the counter and started working on his division homework. For the first time in his life, he didn't know how to do his math by himself, and I could see him getting frustrated. He looked up and asked me for one of the answers. "I'll help you figure it out, but I won't do it for you," I said. He took that to mean I wouldn't help him and his blood began to simmer. He looked back down at his paper and tapped a pencil eraser against his puffed-out cheek.

Blake was standing next to me going on and on about a kid in his class who told him about three bad guys. One was a vampire. "For real Mom, Oscar saw him. And the bad guy threw a knife at Amelia and it landed right by her feet. Is that true Mom?" I told him no, vampires are not real.

"Well Oscar saw one and after the vampire threw the knife at Amelia, Oscar picked it up and threw it back at him. Do you think that could really happen?"

"No Blake, it's not true. Oscar just likes to tell stories."

"Well he also said vampires can cut your neck. Can they?"

Who is this kid?! Sheesh!

During our vampire discussion, Aaron was standing by the pantry begging. "I want chocolate milk. Mom, can you get me some chocolate milk?" I asked Jackson to get the chocolate powder down from the pantry shelf since I was being held hostage by the hungry baby, but he was too busy blowing smoke out his ears to answer me. I told Aaron he'd have to wait.

Aaron dragged a chair from the table to the pantry. "Aaron, just wait. I'll get it for you in a minute," I said. He climbed up on the chair and got the chocolate powder himself. Then he turned the container upside down and shook it to make sure there was plenty inside. It slipped through his fingers, and when it hit the floor the lid popped off, sending a cloud of chocolate sugar billowing into the air.

After the chocolate dust settled and the floor was swept, I took Alex and hid in my bedroom. Jackson finished his homework on his own and brought it for me to look over. He was supposed to read a story problem and write out a number sentence to show the answer. His story problem was something like, *Twelve kids were put into two groups. How many groups were there?* He wrote $6+6 = 12$. It was division homework, so I very calmly told Jackson he had the right idea but the number sentence should read $12/2=6$. All he heard me say was he was wrong. He stomped into his bedroom and shut the door. Then he started shouting at me. "You're WRONG Mom! Six plus six IS twelve. That is RIGHT! YOU are WRONG!"

I descended to his level and hollered back. "Fine Jackson, take it to school and see how your teacher marks it. Maybe then you'll believe me." I should have taken the high road and ignored him, but it's such a lonely path to walk down.

IN THE KITCHEN

I was putting cookie dough balls on a cookie sheet when little Aaron climbed up to the counter and said, "I help!" I handed him a spoon and showed him how to put some dough on the spoon and then onto the pan. He loaded his spoon up with cookie dough and stuck it right in his mouth. I guess he wanted to help me learn how I should have been doing it all along.

———

The kitchen table is an important hub in our house. On it, homework is done, board games are played, and projects are glued together. Under it, forts are made, hide-and-seek is played, and missing binkies are found. The table has naturally suffered a significant amount of wear, but I wasn't about to let Blake purposely scratch it up with a spoon. "Why can't I?" he asked, still scraping the handle back and forth against the tabletop.

"Because it ruins the table, and because it's loud," I said. He locked eyes with me and defiantly stated, "Those aren't good reasons." I walked over and took the spoon from him. He got up and walked away with a chip on his shoulder, no doubt thinking of how he was going to get even.

The kitchen table is where we make plans, frost cupcakes, and courtesy laugh at stale knock-knock jokes (orange you glad I didn't say banana?). We answer life's burning questions, like, "Why do I have to get dressed if we're not going anywhere?" And, "What if Santa brings me the movie I asked for but the wrong disc is in the case?" We get a run-down of what's going on at school, and hear stories about the girl Jackson likes but would rather die than admit he has a crush on.

Last but certainly not least, the table is where we gather for meals. I've been eating dinner every night for my entire life, so I should be a stellar meal planner by now. But more often than not, four-thirty rolls around and I still have no idea what to make. There are steaks, a roast, and chicken breasts in the freezer but none of them will be thawed and ready to cook in time, so those options are out. I open the fridge and stare at a sticky ketchup bottle, lemon juice I don't remember buying, and a single-serve container of half-eaten yogurt without a lid that's been sitting there for a week. I leave the yogurt to live another day, then make my way to the pantry.

No matter how often I organize the pantry shelves, they always look like we just throw boxes and cans of food onto them all helter-skelter, never caring where they land. It's probably time to get rid of the bag of cereal that doesn't even have enough in it to fill one bowl, as well as the empty granola bar box my little dears were too lazy to throw away. *Dinner! Focus!* I don't see anything exciting, so I go back to the fridge and stare some more, as if doing so long enough will make something delicious appear.

I try to remember which one of the kids' seven rotating meals is next in line: grilled cheese sandwiches, pizza, macaroni and cheese, chili, spaghetti, quesadillas, or hot dogs. Nick gets frustrated with me for not making them try new things, but I get frustrated when we live out the same dinner drama every time I serve something new.

It all starts with a baby climbing up my legs, wanting to be held while I'm trying to prepare food. When I don't pick him up, he shimmies between me and the counter and pushes me backwards, trying to get my undivided attention. I carry him into the toy room to play, then run like the wind to get as much done as I can before he's back at my feet. When we finally sit down to eat, a battle over my poor choice in food inevitably ensues. With few exceptions, it can be summed up by a simple yet heated conversation.

Child: I don't want to eat this.

Parent: It's good for your body and it will make you strong.

Child: But I don't like it.

Parent: It's this or nothing. You can't just eat junk all the time. If you don't want what we're having, you can go to bed without dinner.

Child, on the verge of tears: *Can't I just have something else?*

Parent: *You haven't even tried it. Take a bite and you'll see how good it is.*

Child: *I've tried it before and I still don't like it.*

Parent: *Take two bites and then you can have something else.*

Instead of taking a bite, the child pushes his chair away from the table, folds his arms, and sulks. Even if he does try the food on his plate, there's nothing appetizing about sitting across from someone who is gagging on broccoli. Furthermore, everyone is upset and is missing out on funny stories and quality together time. The *hangry* (hungry + angry) child acts out by stirring up trouble and gets punished for not keeping his hands to himself, making things worse. It's a lose-lose situation I'm no longer willing to entertain. So, I make two meals.

However, when the kids treat something they've always eaten like it's suddenly poisonous, it's a different story. "What are those green things in the sauce?" they want to know. *Really kid, we're going to fight about pizza? PIZZA?!*

"They make the sauce yummy," I say. "Otherwise it would just be plain tomato sauce and that's not very good. We've made it this way every time and you've always liked it."

"Tomatoes are in the sauce? Ew. I don't want it."

I always swore I would never use the *starving children in other countries* line on my kids when they wouldn't eat. What did my mom want me to do, send them my plate? Then one night it happened: I opened my mouth and my mother came out. "There are kids in other countries who don't have any food at all, and I made you something you love. Now eat your dinner." The line didn't work, just like it never worked on me, and that was the first and last time I ever used it. The one time Nick tried, Jackson was old enough to counter his argument.

"You should be thankful for your food and eat it. There are lots of kids who are hungry all the time that would love to eat the dinner you're saying is yucky," Nick told the kids.

"Who are they?" Jackson asked.

"They are kids whose parents don't have enough money to feed them," Nick said. "Go ask the kids in China, or Africa, or South America how it feels to be hungry most of the time. Maybe then you'd appreciate what you have."

Jackson replied with, "Well we can't because they wouldn't understand us." By bringing up the language barrier, he perfectly summed up the way I feel about trying to help my kids understand the value of a wholesome meal: like I'm speaking Zulu. With that, the conversation was over.

In order to help dinner be a win-win situation where I felt like the kids ate a reasonably healthy meal and nobody went away hungry or crying, I tried making more nutritious versions of their processed favorites. The first time I made homemade mac and cheese, my kids were so confused.

"What does the box look like?" they asked.

"There is no box."

"Well, what does the cheese look like?"

"It's the normal yellow cheese in the fridge," I said.

"How does the cheese go in? Can we pour it?"

"You don't pour it, you grate it then put it in the pan and it melts."

"How?" they wondered.

I told them to be patient and promised they would love it. Proud of my homemade grub, I was on my way to becoming a domestic diva. I sent the kids to wash up and excitedly anticipated the satisfaction of watching them eat wholesome, homemade pasta. While the boys were in the bathroom, I took a bite and waited for the creamy taste of cheddar goodness to permeate my taste buds. Instead, I turned around and spit it into the sink. The deliciousness I was expecting was grainy and tasteless. I added more salt, which made it edible but far from savory, and served it anyway. Jackson and Blake each took one bite and spit it right back into their bowls; my reaction exactly! After seeing that, Aaron wouldn't even give it a try. I gave up on my diva quest, started buying organic boxed mac and cheese, and called it good.

My kids have started eating a bigger variety of foods as they've gotten older, but getting them to try something new in the first place is like negotiating a nuclear peace treaty. When they finally do, they start by touching the food with their front teeth and without actually tasting it declare they don't like it. Promising them a treat for taking an actual bite and swallowing it would probably work, but that's the exact opposite of what we're trying to accomplish.

Nick and I tried to get Jackson to taste italian sausage by cheering him on and making it exciting. We were clapping and chanting, "Go Jackson, go Jackson, go, go, go!" He smiled and poked a piece of sausage with his fork. Just as he was about to put it in his mouth, Blake brought the momentum to a screeching halt when he chimed in with, "Don't worry Jacks, if it's yucky you can run to the garbage can and spit it out." *Zip it kid!*

I thought we were making progress when Jackson, who only likes peanut butter on his sandwiches (no jam), asked if we could go to Subway. "Sure," I said, delighted that he wanted something different. "What are you going to get?"

"Cheetos!" he said. Sigh.

As incessant as it is, the battle over what to eat (or drink) is trumped by the battle over how the food is served. Aaron was chowing down on a granola bar when he started coughing like he had something caught in his throat. I grabbed a yellow cup, filled it with water, and set it in front of him. In the middle of his coughing fit, he still managed to whine about the cup color.

"I want a green one," he said.

"Hurry and take a drink so you'll stop coughing, then I'll get you a different cup," I said. He shook his head and the frog in his throat croaked, "I want green." I grabbed a green cup and dumped the water from the yellow one into it. What I wanted to do was dump it on his head.

Even when my kids are eating something they love, in their dish of choice, things can still go wrong. Blake poured himself some Froot Loops but they came out too fast and his blue straw bowl was overflowing. I put some back and surprisingly, he didn't have a fit.

"Put a little more back," he said. "I need more room for milk." I took a small handful of cereal and put it back in the box. "Not that much," he said. Then he reached his hand into the cereal box and added exactly three Froot Loops to his bowl. Never underestimate the feng shui of breakfast, or the power it has to create both chaos and peace.

Blake is an early riser, and Jackson is a light sleeper. When Blake gets up, Jackson naturally follows, which makes it hard to sleep in on weekends over the sound of their bickering. "You got the red bowl last time, it's my turn," I hear. Along with, "I get the milk first, I got it out. Give it back," and, "Hey! That was my spoon!"

By the time they finish arguing about bowls and milk, the clash over cartoons begins. "You always pick Ninjago, I want to watch something else," I hear, followed by, "I don't like this show, it's too scary. I'm telling Mom." Once the tattling card is played, I bid farewell to my bed and the day starts.

One Friday night on our way home from a date, Nick and I devised a plan we thought might allow us to sleep in. We stopped and bought cinnamon rolls and donuts and put them on the counter, hoping the kids would discover them and eat without fighting. We must have found some enchanted cinnamon rolls, because not only did we sleep in until 9:00 am, but Jackson, Blake, and Aaron were all watching the same cartoon and we hadn't heard a peep.

Come to think of it, there are a lot of enchanted breakfast foods. We've never gotten into an argument while sitting around the table putting whipped cream and strawberries on our waffles, or powdered sugar on our french toast. Breakfast for dinner it is!

BEDTIME

Me: *Aaron, go lie down and I'll help you get your jammies on.*

He doesn't. I tell him again. He doesn't.

Me: *Aaron, I said go lie down.*

Aaron: *I didn't hear you because you didn't say it loud enough.*

Me: *How loud do I have to say it?*

Aaron: *Like, freaking out.*

Me: *So I have to be freaking out for you to obey?*

Aaron: *Yeah.*

And that, my friends, is called validation.

———

When bedtime dangles the promise of sweet release from the noise of our boisterous home, my impatience grows faster than it does at any other time of the day. Getting the kids ready for bed usually seems to take way longer than necessary, and has a tendency to turn me into a momster. But there are also moments when bedtime is just plain funny.

I once went to turn off Jackson's light and opened the door to see him singing and dancing on his bed. I laughed out loud and scared him. First he jumped, which made it even funnier, then he got embarrassed. I have also caught Blake putting on a concert in his bed. It was four-thirty in the morning and I was on my way to lay Alex in his crib when I noticed Blake's door slightly open and his light on. I walked over to turn it off and saw him softly bouncing around on his bed singing, "Jesus loves me. Jesus loves me." He saw me and started laughing. If you can't sleep, you might as well be happy about it!

There was also the time Blake got out of bed, walked past me without saying a word, and got a Nerf gun from the toy box. He loaded it with darts then turned around and went right back to bed. I guess he needed some harmless foam reinforcements to help him feel safe that night.

One school night when I was in the kitchen eating cantaloupe, Blake had been in bed for about an hour when I heard him coming down the stairs. I could tell it was him by the way he walked, even before I saw his face. "Hi Mom!" he said with a bounce in his step. I looked up and saw that he was dressed and ready for school, proud of himself both for getting ready without help and for beating Jackson to the kitchen.

"Honey, look at you! You buttoned your sweater all by yourself!" I said. "Great job!" Then I had to give him the bad news that it was still night time and I hadn't gone to bed yet. I laughed, he cried. I hugged him and tucked him back into bed and laughed some more.

The occasions when extended bedtime is funny, however, are few and far between. My patience not only diminishes quickly at bedtime, it also has a cut-off time when it becomes non-existent. If my kids aren't in bed when that time hits, the person doing the most whining is me.

Getting kids into pajamas should be easy enough, but with Blake and Aaron wearing the same size, that's not always the case. "Mom, where are my Ninja Turtles pajamas?" Blake asks.

"I folded them and put them in your drawer," I reply from the hallway.

"They're not here Mom," he says.

"I'm ready!" Aaron proudly declares, jumping in front of me with Blake's Ninja Turtles pajamas on.

"Good job buddy, but those are Blake's pajamas so let's find you different ones."

"But he wore them last time and I want a turn," Aaron says.

"I know Aaron, but they're Blake's. What about your minion jammies?"

"Blake can wear my minions," Aaron says as Blake comes barreling out of his room.

"Aaron! Why did you take my pajamas? Get them off!" he shouts.

Oh, for crying out loud! Now there are two kids who are literally crying out loud, and I'm about to start. We sort out the pajama crisis using a little bit of bribery and a little bit of, "Because I said so," but we're just getting started.

Six days out of seven, teeth brushing time consists of the following phrases coming out of my mouth: "Yes, you have to use toothpaste. You know why. That wasn't long enough, use the timer. Do you want the dentist to drill holes in your teeth? Maybe you don't care but I'm the one who pays him, so I'm going to count to 10 and then I will brush your teeth for you." What I should do is record the whole spiel and put it in the boys' bathroom on repeat. Maybe then they'll move along so they don't have to listen to my voice any longer than necessary and I won't have to waste my breath, or smell theirs.

After all the emotional lava that gets spewed out during phases one and two of the bedtime routine, I have to give myself a pep talk to keep going. *I will not raise my voice no matter how many times they get out of bed. I will not even whisper yell. I will hug them and love them and kiss them goodnight like we live in a storybook.*

We gather in one room and say our good stuff, which is where we each say three things we liked about the day. Then we say a prayer, give hugs and kisses, and split up. Blake and Aaron go into their own bedrooms and Jackson goes downstairs to read. He and Blake share a room and if I send Jackson in there before Blake falls asleep, they will be up for hours laughing, fighting, and conspiring against me.

After everyone lands in their designated spot, Nick and I make the rounds to do individual tuck-ins. I go to Aaron first because otherwise, he'll sit in bed and holler at me until I come. "Mom, are you coming? Mom, where are you? Mom, I'm waiting!"

Aaron asks for a drink, even though he had one five minutes earlier, and I tell him to only take one sip so he doesn't have to go to the bathroom in the middle of the night. He says okay and starts downing his water like he crawled across the Sahara to drink it. I try to take the cup but he death grips it and if I pull too hard it will spill. It's not worth the risk of getting his pajamas wet and opening up the Ninja Turtle wound all over again if he has to choose a different pair.

"That was a good sip, huh Mom?" Aaron says when he comes up for air. It was more of a guzzle than a sip, but whatever. He asks for a song and we sing, "You Are My Sunshine," then say goodnight.

I move on to Birthday Cake Blake and he's ready to plan a party. "What are we doing tomorrow Mom? When can we go to Grandma's house again? How old do you have to be to go to Disneyland?" I tell him you have to be eight, but he reminds me his two-year-old cousin went, so that can't be true. I tell him we'll talk about it another time and say goodnight.

"Wait mom, I want to sing you a song," he says and starts right into, "Five Little Monkeys Jumping on the Bed." He sings five little monkeys, then four, then three, then I hear, "Five little monkeys jumping on the bed..."

"Whoa dude, what happened to two monkeys?" I ask.

"Well, I forgot what was next going backwards after three so I had to start over," he replies. I think he was really going for the song that never ends. When he finishes, I say goodnight and turn to leave.

"Mom?"

"What?" Blake looks around the room, trying to think of something else to say. He tells me his hamper is getting full. I tell him to put his clothes in the washer when he gets home from school and say goodnight for the third time.

"Mom?" he says again. I feel a whisper yell forming in my gut. "What?" I say, a little agitated.

"I forgot to put my book in my backpack."

"Do it when you wake up," I tell him and say goodnight. Please heaven, let me get out the door this time.

"Mom?" The whisper yell has moved from my gut to the back of my throat, but I hold it in.

"What?" I say, more agitated than the last time but still somewhat pleasantly.

"Can you check to make sure my alarm is set?" I do it, partly because I love him, but mostly because it will be faster than arguing. I make another attempt at leaving and get all the way to the doorframe before I hear it again.

"Mom?" Blast! I was so close!

I open my mouth and the whisper yell escapes. "Blake! It's late, now go to sleep!"

"I love you," he says. Sucker punch to the gut! I look at his big blue eyes, the ones he could use to get away with murder, and curse my impatience. Well played Blake, well played.

T-R-O-U-B-L-E

Jackson was in the bathroom yelling for me to take him some toilet paper. When I got to the door, Blake was standing outside it with a squirt bottle and a huge grin on his face just waiting for Jackson to come out. Funniest. Thing. Ever!

———

The perfect wall vinyl for my house would be the saying, "The trouble with trouble is it starts out as fun." Fun must have been the only thing on Blake's mind when I looked over just in time to see him standing on a skateboard, on the treadmill, trying to turn it on. Now there's a recipe for an ER visit!

The *real* trouble with trouble is when it starts out as silence. If I haven't heard the kids for a while, I can either enjoy the silence and clean up the mess later or check on them and risk

47

making eye contact. If they are happily playing and our eyes meet, they will suddenly want a snack. And be thirsty. And want me to entertain them.

Until Darin' Aaron came along, I had the luxury of making the choice. But Aaron should not be left to his own devices. He is fast and fearless and in a matter of seconds, he can make a clean room look like an exploded toy factory. He's like a cartoon character who runs full speed ahead while everything behind him blows up and falls apart. When Aaron was two, we tried to outsmart him by putting glass ball ornaments only on the top half of the Christmas tree so he wouldn't break them. He one-upped us by knocking the whole tree down and helping himself.

We've found Aaron hiding in Jackson's room eating the candy from his brother's Easter basket, shoving batteries into the VCR, attempting to swing from the chandelier over the kitchen table, eating deodorant, popping keys off my laptop, sitting on his bed with an open jar of peanut butter (the contents of which were all over his sheet, hands, and face), and hiding in the back of my closet eating chocolate peanut butter cups.

It's like he has a sixth sense that leads him to candy I didn't know we had. When Aaron was two-and-a-half, I was cleaning out the car and let him stand on the middle seat while I vacuumed up wrappers, crumbs, and dehydrated french fries. Then I left him alone for the sixty seconds it took to roll the Shop-Vac back into the garage. In that small window of time, Aaron pulled a Symphony Bar I had forgotten about out of the center console and crumbled it all over the seat. My clean car didn't even last a whole minute.

It was the time I couldn't find Blake or Aaron, however, that they'll never live down. Nick and I were making pizza and realized it had been awfully quiet for far too long, so I called upstairs to see what the kids were doing. Jackson was the only one who responded; Blake and Aaron weren't up there. I did a closet check to see if they were playing hide-and-seek, but didn't find them. They weren't in the backyard or the toy room, so I looked in the front yard and down the street. There was still no sign of them.

When I returned to the house, Nick was standing at the door leading out to the garage. "What are you doing?!" I heard him shout. My husband rarely loses his temper, and when he does, it's nothing like the scene yours truly is capable of making. If Nick was yelling, I knew whatever Blake and Aaron were up to was bad news.

On my way to survey the damage, the smell of gasoline wafted up my nose. Blake had been caught red-handed, with the lawn mower gas can in one hand and a puddle of gas on the ground in front of him. Nick took the can away and told me to get the kids in the house. I took their clothes off, sat them on the floor, and told them not to move.

We cleaned up the mess (heaven forbid you ever need this tip, but gas can be soaked up with flour), then found another surprise waiting inside. Aaron had submerged my wireless computer mouse into a glass of water, rendering it permanently useless. That was the day I started calling him "Aarone

Patrón," because if I ever started drinking, he would be the reason.

The following day, Aaron made another attempt to see if electronics could withstand water by running a remote control through the washing machine. That experiment was a success—it still worked! His love for electronics also made him want to help clean our DVDs. After he saw me breathe on one and use my shirt to wipe off his fingerprints, he starting taking movies straight out of the DVD player and licking them, then rubbing them on his bare belly. *Thanks kid.*

When I'm frustrated and looking for empathy, I rarely find it. Other people seem to think my kids' shenanigans are hilarious. But there are times when I too find them funny, like the time I heard Blake call to me from the kitchen. "Mom! Aaron's trying to butter me up!" There was no way he meant it metaphorically, so I went to see what the fuss was all about. With a mischievous look on his face and a loaded butter knife in hand, Aaron was trying to spread butter on Blake's leg. This is the same child whose footprint I once found in the butter. Maybe that's the source of his talent for slipping away from me.

The only time Aaron isn't going a million miles an hour is when he doesn't feel well and lies on the couch to watch a movie. Even then, he still has plenty of fight in him. When he was two, I took him to Quick Care to get what I thought was an ear infection checked out. He was not about to let the very young nurse take his blood pressure or put an oxygen monitor on his finger.

"If you hold still this won't take long," she kept saying, as if he could hear her soft voice over his screams, or as if he would care even if he could. When she tried to hold his arm in place, he kicked her. I think she actually believed he would let her do it if she asked nicely and tried twelve times.

I myself am no stranger to the pain that little man can inflict. In what started out as a tender moment, Aaron kissed my cheek so I turned my head and told him to kiss the other one. He did, then I leaned my head toward him and said, "Now kiss my forehead." Wait for it . . . wait for it . . . *BAM!* Skull bash. Ouch!

Nick has also felt the pain. I was nursing Alex in the rocking chair when Aaron asked me for a drink of water. "Dad's right there, go hit him up for one," I said. Aaron ran full speed ahead with his fist clenched and punched Nick right below the belt. Trouble often starts out as silence, but in that case, silence would have kept me out if it. Oops!

MOM VS. NATURE

Jackson: Mom, there's a bee on the carpet!

Blake, dancing around and freaking out: A bee! Mom! Hurry!

My kids think all flying bugs are bees, so I got up to shoo the fly; barefoot and unarmed. Sure enough, it was a bee. I first joined in on Blake's dance, and then I killed it.

———

As a mom, I've done a lot of things I said I would never do. Dealing with critters and creepy-crawlies is one of them. People say bugs are more afraid of me than I am of them, but their response to fear is to bite. So when I see one, I follow my response to fear and run. The first time I took care of a spider wasn't until after Jackson was born. Before that, I always found someone with a spine to do it for me. And when I say I took care of a spider, I mean I put a cup over it while screaming, then ran away and waited for Nick to get home and do the rest. Even at that, I only did it because my protective instincts kicked in and I was afraid the spider would bite my baby. Now Jackson is old enough that I can usually bribe him to kill spiders for me, but he doesn't like them either.

"Jacks, grab a shoe and kill that spider," I say.

"No."

"I'll give you a dollar," I offer. It's not enough.

"I'll give you two. Hurry, before it gets away!"

"I don't want to," he says.

I throw out a Hail Mary and offer to buy him a new package of Pokemon cards. He kills the spider and flushes it for the bargain price of only $4.97. I win!

Unfortunately, when Nick is at work and Jackson's at school, I'm on my own. One morning, I returned from taking Aaron and Alex on a walk to discover Alex had dropped his binky somewhere along the way. I unsuccessfully looked for another one in and under his crib, in the toy box, in his high chair, and everywhere in between. Binkies are either everywhere or nowhere; we either have seven, or we have zero. That day, we had zero. Without a binky for Alex to suck on, we would have to forfeit nap time.

Naptime karma is not something I mess with. A missed nap is an unforgiving, vengeful mistake that requires the offender to pay the piper for the rest of the day. Let the baby play on the floor while you make dinner? Ha! His eyes will cry a river as he kicks out his frustration over a mother who dared to tempt fate. After standing and holding the baby for hours on end gets tiresome, don't even think about sitting in a rocking chair to watch TV. He will fall asleep well before bedtime, be impossible to wake up, and then be ready to play in the middle of the night. I learned this with child number one and solemnly swore in the name of everything that is good in this world that from then on, I would honor nap time faithfully. So, we headed to Target.

I opened the car door to buckle the kids in and saw a thick, jet-black spider the size of a quarter climbing up the edge of the seat. It was an episode of Mom vs. Nature, and I had to make a split-second decision: I could either fight a tired baby or a dreadful, eight-legged critter. Apparently I'm more afraid of a baby without a nap than I am of spiders because I set Alex's car seat down on the driveway and pulled off one of my tennis shoes so I could kill it. The spider was faster than I was and dodged my shoe, then disappeared.

I changed into flip-flops in case I needed a weapon in a hurry, then put the kids in the car and prayed the spider wouldn't get one of them. We made it to the store without another sighting and bought two packages of binkies, a binky clip, and a box of diapers. When I opened the back of the car to put the diapers in, the spider was mocking me from the side of the back seat cup holder; as if it knew my flip-flop couldn't flatten it at that angle. The spider stayed obstinately still, but I took a swat anyway. With that, it crawled out of the cup holder and I swatted again. Swing and a miss. Then it started to crawl around the side of the seat where Baby Alex sat, unsuspectingly gumming down a rice cracker.

With my flip-flop raised and my adrenaline pumping, I ran and opened the side door. The spider appeared and I took a fierce whack at it. This time, I got it! It fell from the side of the seat to the floor, but kept crawling. I smashed it a few more times, and finally killed it. I edged its remains into the parking lot with the tip of my shoe and jumped backwards when it landed way too close to my bare toes.

Still suffering from some major heebie-jeebies, I put my flip-flop on and got in the car. "Mom, why were you screaming?" Aaron asked. *Was I?* I was too paralyzed by fear to notice, but when I replayed the scene in my head, I realized I screamed with almost every swat. Good thing nobody heard me, they probably would have called security and said, "There's a crazy lady with only one shoe on screaming in the parking lot, you better make sure her kids are okay."

In that case, I would have shrugged my shoulders and nonchalantly said, "There was a spider."

———

Some forces of nature require professional reinforcements. Can mice even be classified as part of nature? Creatures from *h-e-double-toothpicks* is more like it. A few years ago, we returned from a weeklong Thanksgiving trip and saw a mouse run across our bedroom floor. I freaked out and contemplated taking the family to a hotel until we could contact our pest control company. We hadn't unpacked yet; we could have just thrown the suitcases back in the car.

Nick had to be rational and tell me a hotel wasn't worth paying for, but he was wrong. Even though I had just spent a bunch of money pulling a Black Friday all-nighter, the peace of mind would have been worth every penny.

I called the pest control company the second they opened the following morning and they came out to our house that afternoon. "If you're actually seeing mice, especially upstairs, you probably have a whole family running around on your pipes," the man told me. *Thank you sir, just leave the poison and stop talking.*

He continued, "I also suggest you make sure you don't have anything hanging over the edge of your pantry shelves. Most people don't know mice can jump fairly high. They use overhanging boxes as ledges to jump up to the highest shelf." *For real dude, don't say anything else.*

We sealed off the spot where mice had chewed their way into the house and the pest control guy told us it would take two or three days to stop seeing signs of them. After a week, they should all be dead. For the next two weeks I carried a tennis ball around with me. Each time I walked into a new room I threw it at the wall before I entered, giving any lurking mice time to run away. Then I retrieved the ball and keep it with me in case I needed to throw it at a mouse. If I was alone in a room, I would randomly make a loud noise every few minutes to make sure the mice stayed out. In the kitchen, I would drag a chair across the floor. In carpeted rooms, I shouted arbitrary words like, "Hey!" or "Stay out!"

I never thought there would be a benefit to having a noisy house, but apparently, a few noisy kids a day keep the mice away.

RULES OF THE ROAD

I was trying to distract Aaron from whining about being restrained in his car seat, which he thinks is a straight jacket, by getting him to say different words.

Me: *Aaron, say Mama.*

He said it and I kept him distracted by having him say Dada and Grandma.

Blake, jumping in to help: *Aaron, say She-Hulk.*

Thanks Blake, for supporting the effort.

PART 1: TRAFFIC SCHOOL

Whether you're traveling across town or across state lines, having kids in the car always makes for an adventure. A few simple tricks can make the trip more pleasant, like separating the children who fight most, storing baby wipes under the seat for any possible mishap (even if your baby is a teenager), and putting the baby's car seat on the passenger side so their ear-piercing screams don't have a direct path to your eardrums. But it takes a special kind of driver to create an adventure that involves getting pulled over twice in one hour. Follow this step-by-step guide to join the ranks of the truly talented.

1. How to Get Pulled Over on the Freeway

Drive in the far left lane and when traffic comes to a screeching halt, decide you're not going to sit there for who knows how long and listen to your toddler scream simply because he doesn't want to be in his car seat. Since there are no cars in any of the three lanes between you and the next exit, which is less than fifty feet away, pull out of your lane and drive over to it. Then wait for the discreetly placed motorcycle cop to catch up to you with his siren blaring.

2. How Not to Get a Ticket

Roll down your window and look at the police officer like you have no idea why he pulled you over.

"Do you know why I pulled you over?" he'll ask. Over the screaming eighteen-month-old behind you, say no.

"When you're stopped, people are not expecting you to suddenly pull across three lanes of traffic. That's a great way to cause an accident," he'll say. Your only defense is honesty.

"I'm sorry sir, but I don't know why we stopped. If there's a wreck that's going to have us parked on the freeway for thirty minutes, I'm going to have to listen to my baby scream the entire time. When I saw the exit ahead, that's all I was thinking about. I won't ever do it again."

"Make sure you don't," he'll say sternly and ask for your license and registration. Open your purse and dig through the collection of stray restaurant crayons and half-eaten fruit snack pouches until you find your license. Then open the glove box and remove the pile of napkins keeping the registration cozy. Hand your license and registration the policeman, who will take them and walk back to his motorcycle. While he's there, you get to answer questions from kids who have never before been in the car when one of their parents got pulled over. "Are we going to jail?" is the first thing they'll want to know.

If you're lucky, the officer will return and say, "I'm not going to give you a ticket this time. But please, never do that again."

3. How to Get Pulled Over Again an Hour Later

An hour later, drive down a street you're not familiar with and unintentionally go five miles per hour over the speed limit. Nothing crazy; just enough to catch the radar of another policeman, who's probably been sitting bored for a while now.

4. How to Make Sure You Do Get a Ticket

This time, make sure the backseat screamer is happily

massacring a Pop-Tart and the other kids are mesmerized by the flashing lights behind you. This officer has a real cop car! The kids will be inconveniently quiet and the officer will have no reason to feel sorry for you. You're toast.

———

PART 2: ROAD TRIP HOW-TO

If driving around town with a car full of kids isn't challenging enough for you, take a long road trip. By the time you arrive at your destination, you'll swear you're never going to do it again. That is, until you look at how much plane tickets for the whole family would cost and throw up a little in your mouth. Here are a few tips to help you on your journey. Happy Trails!

1. How to Prepare for a Long Road Trip

Preparing the family for a long road trip is hard work. There are clothes to wash, snacks to buy, electronics to charge, suitcases to pack, and a car to clean out so it can get messed right back up again. If you're an overachiever, you might also want to clean your house before you go. To get the kids out of your hair, send them to pack for themselves. They will excitedly run into their rooms and stuff their suitcases with too many pajamas and not enough socks, forgetting underwear altogether.

It's no big deal, because when the laundry is done you'll need to re-pack their suitcases anyway. Take out the crumpled shirt they wiped their face on after last night's dinner and the yellow Angry Birds flashlight they threw in for the heck of it and replace them with clean clothes and a toothbrush.

This distraction only works until the kids are old enough to catch on. At that point, the eight-year-old will call you out on it. "You're going to take out everything I put in, so just do it for me and I'll keep playing my game," he'll say. Write a list of everything he needs (three long sleeve shirts, five pairs of socks, etc.) and promise to only take out clothes that don't match.

2. How to Leave the Things You Really Need at Home

Before loading up the car, leave the most important things out so they don't get buried. These items include baby bottles and formula, snacks, movies for the kids, extra batteries for their headphones, and your not-sharing-these-with-anyone Ghirardelli chocolate squares. Put them in a bag and leave it out in plain sight. Buckle the kids in, tell them you'll be right back, and run in the house to grab it. On the way to retrieve the bag, you'll notice the light in the toy room is still on. Turn it off, then pass by the bathroom and grab a roll of toilet paper to take with you in case someone needs to blow their nose, or in case the baby needs to unroll it to keep himself entertained. Bypass the reason you went back into the house in the first place and set off on your journey, leaving both the bag of essentials and your sanity on the kitchen counter.

3. How to Make a Pit Stop Take as Long as Possible

Drive to a neighboring state without your husband and stop

at a convenience store for a bathroom break. Tell the four-year-old to stay with you, then watch him run into the Men's bathroom with his two older brothers. You can't go in after him, so nobody will be there to hurry things along.

The four-year-old will have himself a great time repeatedly pulling paper towels out of the dispenser. Instead of telling him enough is enough, the older boys will ball up the towels and slam dunk them into the trash can. If the restroom has a closing door, there's not much you can do. If it has an open entryway, holler as loud as you dare. "Guys, let's go!" Even if they hear you, they will have one last slam dunk contest before they come out.

When the kids beg for a treat, remind them you have all kinds of junk in the car. When they show you what they want, think carefully about your answer. If you say they can pick a treat, instead of getting the one they showed you, they will want to assess their options and walk up and down every aisle. Then they'll ask for a $6 package of Oreos even though you have Chips Ahoy in the car. When they accept the fact that you're not buying cookies that cost double what the grocery store charges, they'll choose a $4 toy with flashing lights and spinning propellers, complete with hard-as-a-rock candy. Set a limit of $2 per child so you can spend the next fifteen minutes telling them how much everything in the store costs. When they finally go back to their original choice, grab it, run to the checkout counter, and hightail it to your car before they change their minds. Or, you could just say no.

Return to the car to find that although there was plenty

of room for everyone when you left the house, blankets, pillows, books, and ear buds have now taken over and there is nowhere to sit. Re-arrange the wreckage and make sure everyone's buckles are secure. Just before you shut the back door, you'll catch a whiff of something foul. Although you just changed the baby when you were in the bathroom, the pungent odor of the bomb he dropped in his diaper has made a comeback.

Don't even think about hauling everyone back inside to use the changing table. Instead, lay the baby on the driver's seat while you change him. Set the diaper on the floor between the seat and the door and put the baby back in his car seat. When you reach for the straps, you'll find that the four-year-old kept himself busy by buckling them all together. Pull the baby out, one-handedly un-do the latches, and try again. While you're at it, break up a fight over whose turn it is for the most coveted DS game and forget about the dirty diaper you left on the floor.

When you get back on the freeway and discover the reason the car still stinks, hopefully you have a plastic bag to wrap the diaper in and suffocate the stench. Otherwise, you're in for round two of trying to get into the Guinness Book of World Records for the longest gas station stop ever; because once you find a place to throw the diaper away, everyone will once again have to go in and go to the bathroom.

Are we there yet?

SOCCER GOALS

T-minus one minute until it was time to leave for Blake's soccer game and he could only find one shin guard. Nick sent him downstairs to see if the other one was in the coat closet. Thirty seconds later, he brought me a dog bone made of two pieces of paper stapled together and stuffed with tissues.

Blake: *Mom, I forgot to show you this dog bone I made at school. See, I even wrote some words on it with my orange marker!*

Me: *Did you find your shin guard?*

Blake: *No, but I did see my backpack in the closet and I remembered the dog bone.*

Time and a place, kid. Time and a place.

———

For six weeks every fall and spring, we drive around with lawn chairs permanently stored in the back of our SUV, keep a ball pump in the diaper bag, and buy Gatorade by the case. It's soccer season, and we eat, sleep, and breathe it. I make sure dinner is ready early on practice days, clench my teeth and make funny faces as I push forever long soccer socks over the tops of shin guards, and grunt as I try to tighten the iron laces on my kids' cleats, which never want to move. I am a quintessential soccer mom, and I have the juice boxes and granola bars to prove it.

Watching games from my lawn chair is always entertaining. Not only do I get to watch my own kids play, but I also get to observe the sideshows going on around me. I laugh at the younger teams who run around in rat packs, all trying to kick the ball at the same time but kicking each other instead. I watch players along the sidelines chase and tackle each other while they wait, and I've even watched a feisty little girl whack her teammate square in the face with a water bottle for no apparent reason. The boy she hit started to cry and since their coach was on the field reffing the rest of their half-pint teammates, both of their mothers ran to separate them.

I'm also surrounded by all kinds of parents. Some yell for their kids to run faster, shoot the ball, pass the ball, or to stop spinning in circles. Some are on cell phones talking business or telling their teenagers to get out of bed and get something done, and some moms are organizing play dates and chatting about the upcoming school carnival.

Being on the field, however, gave me a whole different perspective of the kids and their parents alike. I volunteered to coach Aaron's team his first year because they are always short on volunteers, and Nick was already coaching for Jackson and Blake. Plus, I thought it would be something fun we could do together. If fun is short for *dys-fun-ctional*, I was right.

The kids on my team were cute, to be sure. But as far as soccer skills go, I was in for a reality check. At home, Aaron plays soccer like a maniac. He is in his brothers' faces, blocking their goals, and constantly trying to steal the ball. He kicks it as hard as he can, ignoring the fact that he is aimed right at the fireplace, and that my head is in the way. I thought he would get on the little league field and dominate. Instead, he acted like he'd never kicked a ball before, spent half the time playing in the net, and only lasted about ninety seconds until he was ready for a water break. He was more worried about the post-game treat than anything else. Once he realized he couldn't take the other players down the way he does his brothers, I guess he lost interest.

I had a girl who wore dress-up jewelry to practice and always talked about her hair and shoes. She once stopped in the middle of a game to show me her blue fingernails and tell me about her cousin who painted them. I also had a few criers. One in particular would lie in the middle of the field until his dad carried him off, whether he was hurt or just mad someone else made a goal.

And then there was the parent who sat on the sideline and criticized my every move. He went off about how I didn't know what I was doing, and had never heard the word defense. He ranted with expletives I hoped the kids didn't understand, tempting me to unleash the Silent Speech Giver.

Listen, sir, I did this to spend time with my son and we do practice defense. Your daughter is four, and I guarantee her college scholarship opportunities don't rest on the way she plays little league soccer. Consider volunteering to be the coach next season so you can turn kids who can't even tie their own shoes into professional athletes. Good luck with the criers, I'm pretty sure the league frowns on swearing at preschoolers, so I can't wait to see how you handle it.

But I didn't dignify his diatribe with a verbal response, and continued on as if I hadn't heard him. Though, I considered swapping my "Coach" shirt for one that said, "Parent VOLUNTEER."

Halfway through the season (were we only on game three?!), we played a team that ran us over. I stopped counting their goals at twelve, while we were sporting a big fat zero. I brought an additional player on the field so we had one more than they did, but nothing changed. In the final few minutes, the other coach told his team to stand still and let us kick the ball into the net. Maybe the potty-mouthed dad criticizing my coaching efforts was right.

Aaron's game, if you could call it that, ended and Blake's started shortly after. I was watching Blake dribble down the field when a bubbly little boy from my team came and told me he was still there too because his brother was playing on the field behind us. Then he ran and grabbed his backpack so he could show me all the snacks he brought, his favorite being the bag of Flamin' Hot Cheetos. He sat down next to me and told me about his teacher at preschool, his baby brother, and his dad the policeman; even though I was already well aware of the large man in uniform who often showed up to intimidate me watch his son practice. When his brother's game ended, the boy hopped up and said, "Bye coach! C-ya at practice!" I didn't really care about being the worst mom coach ever anymore, because that made my day.

After letting the judgment of other parents and an ambush by a cluster of four-year-olds get to me, I forgot the real goal of little league soccer. My cute new friend reminded me that it's to give kids a chance make new friends, learn teamwork and sportsmanship, and build character. On that scoreboard, maybe I wasn't so bad after all.

The first time Action Jackson played soccer, there was a curly-haired blonde boy on his team named Quinn. He was not a fast runner, but always gave a hundred percent. I learned that Quinn was born with a defect in his legs and wasn't expected to walk, let alone run without assistance. He defied the odds and ran his little heart out every time he was on the field. The final game of the season rolled around, and Quinn had yet to get a goal. His mom said he had his heart set on scoring just once before the season ended, so she threw in a little extra motivation and told him she'd give him $5 if he got a goal.

When Quinn was in the perfect position to score, his mom shouted, "Five dollars! Shoot the ball!" He kicked it as hard as he could, and it sailed into the net. Every parent with a child on Quinn's team cheered for him like it was the World Cup. He was beaming! A few minutes later, he scored again. We cheered just as loudly as we did the first time and his mom checked her purse to make sure she had a $10 bill.

Quinn's confidence was at an all-time high, and he scored a third time. His fan club went wild. Everyone, except his mother. His mom, who just watched the son she was told would never walk score three goals, wiped tears from her eyes. For Quinn's family, soccer was never about winning or losing. The victory was that he played the game.

THREEATS

Aaron: Mom, can you help me?

Me: Sure, just a minute.

Aaron: Come right now else you'll be in trouble.

Me: Oh yeah? What are you gonna do to me?

Aaron smiles and says: Put you to bed.

YES, PLEASE!

———

When I say, "I'm not going to tell you again," my kids must take me for an idiot. That's exactly what they want—for me to leave them alone. What I really mean is, "If I have to tell you again, it's going to be a yell, not a tell." Saying what I mean is easy enough, but meaning what I say takes a lot more work.

When Jackson was two, instead of walking from the front door to the car, he ran across the front yard and refused to get in. "Jackson, I'm going to count to three and then I'm leaving you here," I said. He stood defiantly in place. I counted to three, then got in the car and drove two houses away. I expected Jackson to have a meltdown, but he was all smiles as he ran and picked up the hose, evidently planning to have himself a water party. I should have learned right then and there that a threat is futile if the child doesn't care about the consequence, but I'm not a very fast learner.

I also have a tendency to dole out punishments that affect me more than they do my kids. Taking away screen time means they follow me around whining that they're bored. "Go outside," I say. But our backyard is only fun when other people come over to play. "Play a game," I suggest.

"Will you play with me Mom?" is the question that always follows. A worthy cause, for sure, but there go my hopes and dreams of getting two baskets of laundry folded before dinner. I could make the whining kids fold laundry, but I read an article on getting children to do their chores and the author was adamant that chores should be viewed as a responsibility, never as a punishment.

It seems like there is an article telling of the negative, lifelong effects of every aspect of discipline, along with an equally reputable article negating everything the first article says. If we're going to mess our kids up no matter what, can't we just sit back and eat Twizzlers and Sixlets while we wait for the world to end? That would definitely be easier, because sometimes following through with threatened punishments is downright heartbreaking.

When he was six, Jackson sneaked a bouncy ball from a friend's house and brought it home in his coat pocket. I talked to him about not taking things that don't belong to us and we walked over to return it. When it happened again, we had the same talk and repeated the process.

A few weeks later, Jackson and Blake were invited to a morning play date at a house they'd never been to before. Later that afternoon, they were going to stay with my parents for a few days until the rest of us joined them for Christmas. They were so excited about going on a trip without Mom and Dad and were bouncing off the walls. I was glad they had something fun to do to distract them for a few hours while I packed their bags. When the boys got home from their play date, Blake told me Jackson put a toy in his pocket and brought it home.

"Jackson, is that true?" I calmly asked.

"No," he replied. But it was written all over his face that he did.

"You're not in trouble, and I'm not mad. But if you took a toy that's not yours we need to give it back," I said. He maintained his innocence and showed me his empty pockets.

"I was going to take it but then I left it there," he said.

"Should I call Matt's mom and ask her to make sure?" I asked.

"She won't find it because I hid it," he said.

"Tell me where you hid it and I'll ask her if it's there."

"No Mom, don't call her."

"Jackson, we've talked about not taking other people's things and Blake wouldn't tell me you brought Matt's toy home if you didn't. If you don't tell me what really happened I'm not going to let you go to Grandma's house today," I said, regretting it the second it came out of my mouth.

"I didn't take it."

"Jackson, this is your last chance," I said, praying he would tell the truth. "If you don't tell me where the toy is, you will stay home from Grandma's house. Think about it before you answer, and tell me what really happened. You're not in trouble, you just need to tell the truth."

"I don't have it," he insisted. My heart sank.

"I'm sorry honey, but you did not tell me the truth. So now you can't go to Grandma's house today." He went in his room and reached under his bed, then brought me the toy.

"Here it is Mom. Let's take it back so I can still go." I wished I never threatened him with staying home from his trip, that he never went on that play date, that Blake never saw him take the toy, and that I had waited until after Christmas to take care of it.

I sat there trying to decide if I was going to go back on what I said, disgusted with myself for saying it in the first place. We had a lesson in my parenting class that very week about how following through with our threats teaches our kids to believe the things we say. On the flip side, by not following through, we actually teach them not to believe us. I knew if I let him go to Grandma's he wouldn't think lying was a big deal, or take my threats seriously.

"Jackson, I gave you lots of chances, and I told you twice if you didn't tell the truth you would have to stay home. So now you can't go."

His face fell. I was sick to my stomach and heartbroken for the little guy.

"Does Blake still get to go?" he asked.

"Yes," I said.

"I'll never do it again," he promised

"I hope you don't bud, but if I let you go, then it would mean I wasn't telling the truth when I said you would have to stay home. So Blake is going to go by himself and you can wait and go with Mom and Dad and Aaron in a few days."

He walked into his room, shut the door, and cried. I walked into my room, shut the door, and cried. I called Nick, hoping he would help me justify letting Jackson go anyway. Nick told me we had to follow through with my decision for all the reasons I already knew.

There are so many better ways I could have handled that situation. I knew Jackson wasn't telling the truth, and I mistakenly thought the threat of the biggest punishment I could think of would remedy that. But he was more afraid of getting in trouble in that moment than anything else. And I probably had taught him not to believe me by not following through with threats I had made in the past.

Why did I decide to follow through on the biggest one of all, especially when he was truly sorry? He did ultimately bring me the toy. I could have shown some mercy and let him give it back and still go on his trip. I was punishing myself most because instead of getting a break, I was going to have a sad little boy on my heels for the next few days. I am my own worst enemy.

I doubt I'll ever know exactly where the cutoff line for *one more chance* should be drawn, and I don't love being the one to draw it. Jackson never took anything that wasn't his again, but it was a hard lesson to live out—for both of us.

A FOUR-LETTER WORD

I found Aaron's preschool orientation packet a few months after preschool started and noticed a tiny yellow paper clip in the top corner. Attached was a flyer saying his class had show and tell every Tuesday. I swear I had never seen that paper before.

> **Me:** *Aaron, do you have show and tell at school sometimes?*
>
> **Aaron:** *Yeah, the other kids bring stuff in their backpacks.*
>
> **Me:** *Do you want to take something today?*
>
> **Aaron:** *Yeah, I've been wanting to do that! It will be so fun!*

He jumped up and ran to find something cool to share while I filled out my application for mother of the year.

———

"Fail" is a four-letter word that makes me cringe. I don't like letting myself down, and I certainly don't like letting other people down. As a kindergartner, Jackson was excited for free dress day at school so he could show off his new Super Mario Bros. shirt. For days leading up to it, he reminded me every night. "Mom, on Friday, we don't have to wear our uniforms! I'm wearing my Mario shirt!" On Friday morning, he woke up and looked through his drawer.

"Mom, where's my shirt?" he asked.

"It's in the . . ." Dang it! I forgot to put the clothes in the dryer. "It's in the washer, but I'll put it in the dryer right now and it should be ready by the time you go," I said. His shirt was not even close to dry by the time he had to leave, so he chose a different one. It would have been so easy for me to put his shirt in the dryer the night before, but I just plain forgot. Fail!

My kids have a special talent for letting me know when I don't measure up, as evidenced by the following conversation:

Blake: *Mom, will you get me that game that's way up high?*

Me: *Sure!*

Blake: *Thanks Mom, you're the best. Jackson, is Mom the best?*

Jackson: No, I think Grandma is.

Blake: No, I think Dad is.

Jackson: Yeah, Dad. Yeah, yeah, it's Dad.

I never had a chance. One rainy afternoon, I suggested building a fort together. My boys had no confidence in my abilities. "What if you don't do a good job?" Jackson said. "Yeah, let's just wait for Dad," Blake said in agreement. We played GeoTrax instead.

Another time, I was making cookies for a sick friend and Jackson asked me what they were for. I told him and he said, "I thought you have to eat good stuff when you're sick so you get better, not treats." Do as I say, child, not as I do.

When we read as a family, Nick and I ask the kids questions to make sure they understand the story. One night, we took turns telling stories we made up instead of reading from a book. Blake's story was about five bears. In true Blake story-telling fashion, his story dragged on and on. After the bears had climbed trees, eaten pizza, and driven tractors, I zoned out.

"So Mom, were there birds in my story?" Blake asked. I obviously missed something.

"Yep, birds," I said.

"No Mom, they were bears!" he replied. My own tactic had been used against me. That night the word "bear" also became a four-letter word.

As if I'm not already hard enough on myself, there are

plenty of people who brazenly point out the things I'm doing wrong at the park, in restaurants, and in line at Old Navy.

Alex was about six months old when my brother brought his girlfriend over meet us. It was summer and Nick, Jackson, and Blake took our guests four-wheeling for the day. They used our SUV to pull the trailer, so my brother left me his car keys in case I needed to go somewhere. I forgot I was without a house key and accidentally locked Aaron, Alex, and myself out. Nick didn't have cell phone service so I couldn't find out how long they'd be gone, which left us with time to kill. It also left us painfully aware that the air conditioner in my brother's car was broken.

We went to Target and Costco, then I nursed Alex in the hot car and we headed to Old Navy. Aaron picked out a new superhero shirt while I held and tried to comfort an exhausted baby, but Alex wouldn't stop crying. He was so ready to be home, which made two of us. There was only one checkout lane open and while we waited in line, Alex continued to cry. The two women standing behind were quick to let me know I was an unfit mother.

"That's why I'm never having kids," one said to the other, in a voice loud enough to make sure everyone in the store knew how much of a nuisance my baby was. "People who can't handle them shouldn't either."

I bit my lip so I wouldn't turn around and snap at them like an angry alligator at the watering hole. By the time it was my turn to pay, the Silent Speech Giver had told them off ten times over.

My baby is dressed, his diaper is clean, and he is fed. I'm holding him in my arms, and he won't take his binky. We are locked out of the house and he is exhausted. If you think because a baby cries he is not being taken care of, you're right, you shouldn't have children. And if you need another reason, come closer. He just ate so I'm sure he'll spit up any second.

Oh, how I wished I was as brave as they were and dared to pop off to a perfect stranger. I said nothing, paid for Aaron's shirt, and left. I did wonder if I should have said something though, because they had no idea where I was coming from. Perhaps I could have taught them not to judge situations they know nothing about. But I'm also guilty of that, so even though I didn't say anything, the lesson wasn't wasted on me.

No matter what anyone else says, nothing makes me feel more like a failure than feeling like my own kids don't like me. I've heard that's the mark of a good parent, but it certainly doesn't feel like one. The summer before he entered third grade, Jackson started to think everything I said and did was so dumb. Newsflash: boys can roll their eyes just as well as girls can, and just as often. His favorite things to say to me were, "That's not how you do it," and, "You don't know Mom."

When my kids start fighting in the car, I distract them by making up silly songs. "Blake the snake is awake. Blake the snake, lives by the lake! Scarin' Aaron, let's get some music blarin'. Action Jackson . . ."

"Stop being weird," Jackson says before I get to the part where he solves a fraction.

Jackson has always liked Nick better, even as a baby. The older he gets, the more blatant his parental preference becomes. I will never be the soccer coach or player his dad is, I'll never be able to beat the video games his dad can, and I will never drive a truck or teach him about football the way his dad does.

I am the robot mother who makes his lunches. I am the delivery service that drives the forty-five minute round trip to take his ChapStick to the school because his teacher called and said his lips were cracked and bleeding. ChapStick he told me was in his backpack that very morning, no less. I am the launderer who washes his soccer jersey so he can wear it every single afternoon without getting some sort of toxic fungal build-up, and I am the annoying homework enforcer. Bo-ring!

The night before Jackson's first third grade spelling test, I offered to help him study his words. This is how it went . . .

Jackson: I don't need to, I already know them all.

Me: I want to make sure. Spell lettuce.

Jackson: L-e-t-t-u-s

Me: Almost, try again.

Jackson: L-e-t-t-i-c

Me: Not quite. Do you want me to tell you how?

Jackson: I already know how.

Me: So far you haven't gotten it right, so . . .

Jackson: That's because I don't want to do this. So I'm going to keep spelling it wrong until you let me stop.

Me: No dude. Spell it right.

Jackson: L-e-t-t-y-s

Me: Jackson, you're not going to soccer practice until we're done.

He then spelled it correctly and didn't miss a single word on the rest of his list.

Me, the next morning: Jackson, I just want you to spell one word for me before your test today. Spell lettuce.

He rolled his eyes.

Me: Just do one.

Jackson: O-n-e.

How's that for making sure he had the final say? That same weekend, Jackson was sitting at the table doing a puzzle when I looked over his shoulder to check it out. "Don't touch it Mom, I'm doing it myself," he said. Not two minutes later, Nick came downstairs and sat at the table. "Dad, do you want to do my puzzle with me?" Jackson asked him. Ouch. After dinner, I invited Jackson to go on a bike ride with me, but he didn't want to. Sometimes I feel like the president of a club

I'm not allowed to join. I schedule their events and plan their meals, but when they spontaneously decide to hold a meeting, the all-boy club is exactly that. What does it take to get another girl around here?

I'm admittedly envious of my friends who have daughters to take to the nail salon, play dress up and hair stylist with, and take shopping. That day, I was jealousy incarnate. I hope one day my nieces go extreme teenager on their parents and don't want to be anywhere near them. They can come to my house and I will spoil them rotten. Manicures and milk shakes, anyone?

———

Jackson is what I call my "me child." For better or worse, our personalities and tempers are the same. The better is that he picks up on things quickly, loves to read, and has a great memory. The worse is that he expects perfection, both from himself and others, but has little patience in waiting for results. Of course, perfection is in the eye of the beholder, and the times we butt heads most are the times we both think our way is the only way.

I got tired of butting heads with Jackson, and even more tired of feeling like he never wanted to be around me. Something had to change. If it meant he could stand to be in the same room as his nagging mother, I was no longer going to check his math homework or make him practice his spelling words. If his answers were incorrect, he would figure it out at school.

Within days of me getting out of Jackson's business, he came around. Letting my "me child" control his own life was the key. It took me months and a few pity parties to unlock the simple truth that he wants to call the shots and does not want to be around someone who insists on calling them for him. That sounds exactly like someone else I know—go figure!

I also realized I don't have to be good at soccer to have a conversation with Jackson about it. All I have to do is ask him if there are any good matches coming up and he tells me all about which teams will be playing, who their best players are, and everything else he knows about them. And I definitely don't need any prequalifications to go to Jackson's games and be his biggest cheerleader, especially when he scores a goal with his left foot, because nobody else knows how hard he's worked to be able to. I fail when I don't spend time on things that are important to him; but if I make a sincere effort, he usually returns the favor.

BOYS WILL BE BOYS

Aaron, while watching Alex get his diaper changed: I have one of those in my diaper too.

Me: One of what?

Aaron: One of those, like Alex.

Anatomy 101 at our house.

———

"The itsy bitsy spider went up the water spout, down came the . . ." *SMACK!* With no warning whatsoever, a softball hit me in the head.

"Blake! Why did you throw that at Mommy's head?" I asked him.

"Play catch!" his two-year-old voice replied. It was

definitely the fastest way to get my attention, but a heads up would have been appreciated!

A house full of boys is constantly filled with the echoes of a game of catch or hide-and-seek, a growling match, a soccer shoot-out, or a basketball game. When I wake up each morning, the possibilities of who I might be are endless. I could be a goalie, a referee, a monster, an umpire, or Luigi (nobody ever lets me be Mario).

Our house is also full of a whole lot of boy gross, which seems to faze only me. My kids don't see a problem with wearing dirty clothes and stinky socks as long as they can get outside as quickly as possible. And get serious Mom, there's no reason to take a bath if there's no visible dirt. Never mind that the boys smell like they slept in a dumpster, or that their stiff hair could pass for a Brillo pad. I've gotten used to a lot of things that once made my stomach turn, but some things will always be disgusting.

I asked Aaron to bring me a tissue, so he ran to the bathroom and ripped off some toilet paper. On his way back, he stopped and blew his nose with it. Then he proudly offered it to me and said, "Here Mommy!" *Um, thanks?*

What's worse than boys not comprehending nastiness is how hilarious they think it is. When Aaron was being potty trained, Nick and I cheered for him every time he used the toilet, as did his two older brothers. We clapped, gave him high fives, did victory dances, the whole nine yards. One morning, we had to pick Jackson and Blake up from a basketball workshop and I sent Aaron to the bathroom before we got in the car. I made a big deal about how great he did, then told him to flush the toilet and wash his hands while I stepped away to get Alex ready.

As soon as Jackson and Blake got in the car, Aaron loudly announced, "Guys! I went potty in the toilet!" They congratulated him and he said, "I saved it so you could see." They all laughed and thought it was the funniest thing ever. At least he left his business in the toilet instead of putting it right under my nose, which has also happened.

One summer morning, after being up with Alex all night, I woke to little feet running toward my bedroom. Even though he saw me in bed, with my eyes closed, Blake came in and talked to me anyway.

"Mom?" I pretended to stay asleep and hoped if I ignored him, he would go away. No such luck.

"Mom! Aaron spilled pretzels on the floor." That was so not worth waking me up for. I told Blake to leave the mess and I'd clean it up later. I was almost back to sleep when I heard a different pair of munchkin feet coming to make sure I didn't make it back to dreamland. This time it was Aaron, who by then was potty trained but still wore diapers to bed.

"Mom, can you put my diaper back on me?" he asked, standing half-naked next to my bed.

"No honey, it's time for undies. Go get some out of your drawer and put them on. Make sure you get them out of your drawer, not out of the hamper," I said with my eyes still closed.

Aaron took his open, wet diaper and plopped it down on my pillow, right in front of my face. I opened my eyes to see his naked little behind running for the door. I sat up and closed the diaper, then threw it in his direction but wasn't fast enough to bop him.

With a love of all things sticky and stinky also comes an aversion to affection that starts about the same time as preschool. Blake was particularly determined never to let a kiss stay on his cheek for more than a second, always wiping it off with an expression of disgust. One night after he was asleep, I tiptoed to the side of his bed and kissed his forehead. Blake opened his eyes and pulled his blanket up over his face, using it to wipe off the kiss. Not even sleep could keep a kiss on him.

A few days later, Aaron was sitting on the Love Sac watching a movie. Blake sat next to him and Aaron started to cry.

"Blake, leave your brother alone," I said.

"I'm just trying to hug him and he won't let me," Blake said. *Well, kid, how does it feel?*

The word "boy" is usually synonymous with the word, "rowdy." I don't pay much attention to unexplained bruises that could have come from balls, cleats, wall corners, trampoline bars, or attempted stunts. I have routinely cleaned and bandaged my share of skinned knees, bleeding wounds, and invisible owies only a Band-Aid can fix. There are times, though, that I hold my breath and wait to see how an injury is going to shake out.

Jackson took a ball to the face at an indoor soccer game that knocked him flat. To everyone's amazement, without missing a beat, he jumped right up and started running again. The mom standing next to me was especially worried about

Jackson and told the coach to make sure he was okay. The coach let the play continue, and she repeated her request.

"I think he's okay," I said to her. "Now that he knows it won't kill him if he gets hit with the ball, he might be more aggressive." From the look on her face, I'm pretty sure she thought I was evil.

Other times, I can't get to the injured child fast enough. After school, Jackson and Blake like to jump out of the car when we drop their friends off (who just live down the street and around the corner) and race me home. If they run really fast, they can usually beat me. One afternoon Blake was running as fast as his little legs could take him when I caught up to him going two miles per hour. He looked over and waved at me with a huge grin on his face, and kept watching me as he ran. I saw a set of mailboxes a few feet in front of him, but he didn't.

"Blake! Watch out!" I rolled down the window and shouted. He turned his head just in time to bash into the side of one of the metal mailboxes, right at eye level. I pulled over and ran to him, expecting to find him bleeding out his eyeballs. Luckily, he scraped his cheek just under his eye and there wasn't any blood. Once I realized we weren't headed to the hospital, I wished I had it on video. Okay, so maybe I am a little bit evil.

Some boy behavior is innate, but some is learned. Aaron asked for some orange juice while I was in the middle of making lunch, so I told him he'd have to wait. He didn't like that answer, so he climbed down from his stool and got it out of the fridge himself.

"I need a cup, Mom," he said.

"I know bud, set the juice on the counter and let me finish making your sandwich. I can only do one thing at a time."

Blake piped in and said, "Nuh-uh Mom, you can do six." I assured him I couldn't, to which he replied, "Yeah you can, I've seen you." And I always thought my mechanical mommy efforts went un-noticed. It was time to lower some expectations. When I turned my back, Aaron unscrewed the orange juice lid and took a drink straight from the container.

"Aaron, we don't do that. It gets germs in the juice," I said.

"But I want to do it how Daddy does it," he replied. Jackson laughed out loud and told me Nick also drinks from the milk container. He was so busted! Now if my kids could learn to copy the way their dad does yard work, we'd be set!

HUSBAND HACKS

Nick and I were making buttermilk syrup for the first time. I started asking him to read me the directions but stopped mid-sentence to mix something.

Me: Honey, can you read me . . .

Nick: That is for sure the hardest thing you have ever asked me to do.

———

If Nick rode into my life on a white horse and wearing shining armor, I still wouldn't have paid him any more attention than I did when we first met, which was essentially none. In high school, I got asked on one date. Another girl told me the boy only asked me to go with him because the girl he wanted to take couldn't and his friends were still making him pay his share for the group date. I found out she was right, and felt stupid the whole night.

When I went to college, it was two years before someone asked me on a date. Again, I found out I wasn't his first choice, but his friend *like-liked* my roommate so they thought if we all went on a double date, there was a better chance she'd say yes. (If you are a single male and randomly happen to be reading my mommy memoir, be advised that in situations like these the girl WILL find out!) That wasn't the only date I went on in college, but by the time I graduated, the total number of people I had gone out with more than once was two.

I spent a lot of time during high school and college helping my friends get ready for dates and dances I wasn't invited to and even more time wondering why. When I moved into the apartment complex where Nick lived, I had finally figured out how to be happy with myself whether boys liked me or not and was having the time of my life hanging out with my friends. I even had a trip to Italy in the works, and had no interest in letting the dating scene mess with my head, my heart, or my fun.

The first time I met Nick, one of my roommates (who he was already friends with) passed him on the sidewalk and invited him to come in. He introduced himself to me and asked my name. He asked me a few other questions but I didn't say much, or ask him anything in return. He later told me with my one-word answers, he could tell I wasn't very interested in the conversation. I'm glad he caught on; I just wanted to go upstairs and change out of my skirt.

We saw each other again at a party the following weekend and Nick came over to say hello. I was nice to him, but again, didn't say much. All I remember talking about was how I wished they had ice cream there. A few days later, Nick called to see if I wanted to go get some ice cream with him but I wasn't home. When I saw the message on the whiteboard, I erased it without returning his call. He called again that same night, and I accepted his invitation but made my roommate go with us. Why Nick ever talked to me again after that I have no idea.

While we were eating, I mentioned I liked to go running (ah, the good old days), but hadn't gone for a while because it was winter and I wasn't a fan of having my lungs hurt for days after running in the cold. Nick told me there was an indoor track close by and if I wanted to check it out, he'd go with me. I wasn't about to open myself up to rejection, but a little exercise couldn't hurt anything, so I said okay.

Before my anti-dating crusade, I would have at least tried to look cute before he picked me up. But running wasn't a date, and I wasn't trying to impress anyone, so I put my hair in a ponytail and wore my most comfortable, unattractive gym clothes. Nick opened the car door for me and I was surprised since we weren't going anywhere special, but I was admittedly impressed.

After our first run, we scheduled another one, and soon became regular running buddies. My roommates kept telling me Nick liked me and I tried to tell them we were just workout friends, but I knew they were right, and it scared me to death. What if I let him break down the *I don't care if you like me or not* wall I worked so hard to build and he broke my heart?

Nick didn't know about the battle going on in my head, yet still put up a heck of a fight, chipping away at my wall one chivalrous act at a time. He was a perfect gentleman every time we went to the track, always coming to the door to pick me up and walking me to the door after we got back. He also made me laugh a lot, and I soon upgraded him from, "not a chance" to "okay, maybe."

Nick either had impeccable timing or noticed my gym clothes got a makeover, because as soon as I trusted him enough to step out of the friend zone, he asked me during a post-run cool-down if I'd like to go to a basketball game with him later that same evening. By the time I got home, I only had a half hour to get ready. I was really hungry, but a shower was not optional, so I skipped the snack.

It's funny what starting to like someone does to a person. Nick usually saw me sans-makeup and dripping sweat with my hair matted to my head. Now all of the sudden I was worried about what I looked like? I finished getting ready with five minutes to spare and headed downstairs intending to grab an apple from the fridge. When I stepped into the living room, Nick was sitting on the couch. My roommate let him in on her way out, but didn't bother to tell me.

"Oh dang-it, you're here," I said. I had an immediate, *Did I say that out loud?* moment and tried to remove my foot from my mouth by explaining my way out of it. "I mean, I was going to grab a quick snack before you came but you're already here." Was I trying to sabotage myself? Maybe.

"Go ahead, I'm happy to wait," he said. I grabbed a granola bar and we went on our way. I didn't watch much of the game, but instead spent the evening laughing at Nick's dance moves and random jokes. That night when he walked me to the door, he gave me a hug I didn't want to let go of, and my crusade was officially over.

Nick was kind, thoughtful, intelligent, funny, and spent Sunday afternoons volunteering at a nursing home: the perfect mix to turn my love-reluctant self into a love-struck fool. Once my heart told my brain to be quiet so I could admit to myself that I had liked Nick all along, I fell fast and I fell hard. Falling in love with Nick made me grateful I spent so many Saturday nights alone, because they meant I was free to be his.

———

After our wedding bells stopped ringing, it didn't take me long to realize even men who may as well have dropped out of a Jane Austen novel can't read minds, or think like women. Life would be easier if they could, but it would also be quite boring. After all, Nick was the one clever enough to keep a special gift secret by slowly getting small amounts of cash back at the grocery store and selling some of his books so he could pay cash and I wouldn't know he spent any money. And it was him who, even after ten years of marriage, carried flowers on a plane home from Seattle to say, "I'm happy to be back with you."

Yet in day-to-day life, I still get frustrated by the differences in the way male and female brains are wired; especially after throwing kids into the mix. Fortunately, I have learned a few husband hacks to help bridge the gap.

1. Give Him Wrapping Paper and Candy Bars

Christmas shopping is infinitely less cumbersome than it used to be thanks to the Internet. My favorite thing about shopping online is not having to drive at a snail's pace behind people leaving the mall like a creepy stalker so I can claim their parking spot. But even gifts delivered right to the doorstep still need to be wrapped, and I'm not about to do it alone!

To get my man to help wrap Christmas presents, I wait until the kids are asleep and then turn on a movie he likes. We sit on the floor and I hand him a roll of wrapping paper, some scissors, and a roll of tape. Then I set a bowl of mini candy bars next to him for motivation. I organize the gifts into one large garbage bag per child, so all Nick has to do is wrap them and put them back in the same bag. I also give him the youngest child's presents. That way if they look like a three-year-old wrapped them, that's who they're for anyway.

Halfway through the wrapping session, when the candy is gone and my husband is wearing down, I say something like, "I thought I bought more than this but now it doesn't look like much. I should probably buy a few more gifts for each kid." Nick goes on about how the kids hardly ever play with the toys they already have and tells me not to buy anything else. I shrug my shoulders and refill the candy bowl and he keeps wrapping, glad he was there to keep me from spending more money.

If there's no way on this green earth your husband is going to wrap presents, choose an afternoon to send him to the theater with the kids instead. He can have Disney songs stuck in his head while you watch *Anne of Green Gables* and eat all the candy bars yourself.

2. Birthday Matters

A few months after we were married, Nick called me at work to say there was a surprise waiting for me in the fridge. He wouldn't give me any hints, so I spent the rest of the day excited to get home and see what it was. I thought of everything from dinner to cheesecake to flowers. I got home and eagerly opened the fridge to find the eyes of two dead fish Nick caught that morning staring right back at me. Granted, it wasn't my birthday, but to avoid any more surprises like this, especially on my birthday, I take matters into my own hands.

If I want a party, I plan one for myself. If there's something I've been eyeing, I tell the hubs he's off the hook and go buy it. The year Nick was out of town on my birthday, I took the day off from work and went to lunch with the kids at Café Rio, took them to dinner at Taco Bell, and topped it off with dessert from Cold Stone. Then I got them a sitter and went out with my friends. It might as well have been all of our birthdays, we had so much fun!

I've planned everything from a quiet night with Nick to dinner out with other couples to miniature golfing with the kids; it just depends on what I feel like. But I guarantee what I'm not feeling is disappointed that my husband didn't telepathically plan the party I wanted, or buy me the gift I never told him about.

3. Handy (Wo)Man

If I've repeatedly asked my husband to fix something and he hasn't had time, I have options. If he's not home, I watch a YouTube how-to video and start the project myself. If the attempt is successful, I've learned a new skill! If I get half way through and realize I'm making the problem worse, I leave the repair in its disastrous state. When Nick gets home, he makes time to do it properly.

Some things, however, should not be messed with. When our dishwasher wasn't draining, I did some e-search and thought I could fix it myself. I started to take it apart and had visions of taking a selfie in front of the repaired dishwasher then posting it as a status update with the caption, "I'm not just a pretty face you know!" Instead, I pulled a little too hard on one of the pieces and broke it. The look on my face wasn't so pretty when the piece snapped in half.

If my husband is home, I grab his tools and make sure he sees I'm about to use them. He inevitably follows me and tries to take over. I say something like, "It's okay honey, I can do it," and make him think I'm actually going to until he invites me to leave. Done and done!

4. Buy Him Tickets

For our first Valentine's Day, I bought Nick tickets to an NBA game. I had them sent to my office, which was the first time I had ever received mail there. My male co-worker brought me the envelope and was naturally curious about what was inside. I told him I didn't know what to get Nick for Valentine's Day, but I knew he loved sports, so I bought him tickets to a basketball game. My co-worker asked me if I would call his wife and tell her to do the same. I didn't realize it would be such a popular idea until word spread and several other male co-workers complimented me on the idea.

Tickets are the man gift jackpot, especially if your man is a sports fan. There are even gift certificates available for him to try his hand at curling if you have a venue nearby. If he isn't into sports, you can purchase tickets to concerts, comedy clubs, rodeos, Monster Truck Rallies, or art exhibits. If all else fails, go with movie tickets. Even though they may seem a bit cliché, movie tickets are still a step forward in the direction of, "Let's get out of here together." Just be sure to let him pick the movie!

5. The Silent Treatment

When I'm mad at my husband, who we have established can't read my mind, choosing not to talk to him instead of telling him what I'm thinking makes no sense whatsoever. But sometimes, I do it anyway. Then I walk around replaying the scene of whatever ticked me off over and over in my mind, getting more upset each time. In the end, we talk it out but I've lost an hour or two of my life I'll never get back.

Another funny thing about the silent treatment is sometimes, Nick doesn't even know he's getting it. If anything, he probably likes it. The first time I ever tried it, he had already apologized and moved on. But I was still upset, so I went upstairs and plotted revenge, which consisted mostly of not talking to him.

Once Nick finally realized I was still hurling surliness in his direction, he said, "Whenever you're frustrated with me, just know I don't try to make you mad. I never have and never will do anything that starts with me thinking, 'This will make Amber mad, but I'm going to do it anyway.' I'm still learning." I keep that little gem around to help me remember he can't, in fact, read my mind.

6. Write It Down

When a man leaves the house, he kisses his wife and says, "Bye honey." The only thing he might need to worry about is grabbing a jacket. When a woman leaves the house, it starts with a speech.

"There are hot dogs in the fridge and buns on the counter for dinner. If the kids don't want those, there's leftover spaghetti. Or you can take them to Wendy's. If you do, don't let Jackson drink root beer because it hurts his stomach. Be sure Aaron goes to the bathroom before bed. There are warm pajamas for him in the dryer. Don't let him wear shorts or he'll get cold. Babe, are you listening?"

"I heard everything you said," Nick assures me.

"Feed Alex at 8:15. There are pureed sweet potatoes in the fridge. If they're too thick, mix them with water before you warm them up. If he starts to fall asleep early, feed him early but do not let him go to sleep without eating. Unless you want to get up with him at 5am."

Nick tells me he's managed to keep the kids alive every other time I've left the house and to leave already. At 8:00 my cell phone rings. "What did you say Alex should eat?"

If I don't put my pre-exit speech in writing, I end up repeating it over the course of several phone calls. Or, I end up writing it down anyway in the form of intermittent text messages. Of course, I could also choose to be okay with things not being done in the control freak way I want them. The kids always have tons of fun in the land of *Mom Never Lets Us Do This*, and my husband is more willing to let me leave when he's not being micromanaged from the mysterious goings-on of girls' night out.

7. Wake Him Up

Toward the end of my pregnancy with Alex, I told Nick I wasn't excited about the months of middle-of-the-night rendezvous the new baby and I were soon to have. "It didn't take that long for the other kids to sleep all night. Maybe this one will be the same," Nick said.

Did we live in the same house? The itchy, irritating eczema on Blake's face kept him up most of the night for nine months. How did Nick not hear him cry, or feel me get in and out of bed several times every night? Some mornings I had been asleep for all of forty-five minutes when the alarm went off. "Did Blake sleep all night?" Nick dared to ask, making me want to kick him. Hard. I contemplated purchasing a fog horn to wake him up with every time the baby needed help, but that would have also woken up the two-year-old, and I'd rather re-live seventh grade than have him join the party.

It's a scientific fact (one I learned way too late) that a crying baby isn't even one of the top ten sounds that wake a man[1]. However, it is the number one sound for women, even if the crying child isn't theirs. Had I known all along, I wouldn't have laid awake hoping Nick would get out of bed and get the kid. Sometimes, I was sure he was just pretending to be asleep, challenging me to a contest to see who would wait it out the longest.

If I want my husband to get out of bed and give the baby a bottle, I have to wake him up. Waking him takes several attempts because he goes right back to sleep after each one. After a few tries, I touch my freezing cold feet to his bare skin to get him to move. When he finally sits up, I steal his pillow so he no longer has a comfortable place to lay. "It's your turn," I mumble as I put his pillow under my head and go to sleep. I only did this on weekends when Nick didn't have to work, but for those two days I felt like a million bucks!

---

1. "When Daddy Goes Deaf: How Men Really DON'T Hear Babies Crying While Asleep" DailyMail.com. November 30, 2009. Accessed May 1, 2015.

8. Give Him Choices

The man brain doesn't always recognize mom needs help until she is either yelling or crying, so I have learned to ask for help before becoming the poster child for the benefits of waterproof mascara. I simply tell Nick what needs to be done and give him a choice: he can either go buy milk or put the baby to bed. If he opts for the baby, he'll undoubtedly choose the one pair of pajamas that accidentally got left in the drawer instead of being thrown into the too small bin. But that's okay because I get to buy myself a treat on my milk run and eat it without having to share. I also get to listen to my favorite radio station instead of sing-a-long ABCs all the way home. Score!

9. Give Him the Benefit of the Doubt

The night of Aaron's preschool orientation, Nick had to work later than usual so the welcome relief I get when he takes Alex while I make dinner didn't come. Thus, I was browning hamburger and shredding cheese with a screaming baby on the floor and the noise of rowdy little kids echoing all around me. Nick got home just in time to eat, and after dinner, I had to take Aaron to meet his new teacher.

"You're taking the baby too, right?" Nick asked as I was trying to get Aaron to keep his leg straight so I could put his shoe on his foot.

Heck no, I thought. *I need a break!* But I could tell Nick wanted me to, so I got Alex ready and the Silent Speech Giver went crazy. *I'm with him all day every day. You've only seen him for two seconds today. I'll take him with me but when we get home, he's yours. You know, for the twenty minutes between then and bedtime.*

When we got home, I could see a piece of humble pie waiting for me as I noticed the front lawn had been freshly mowed. I ate another piece when I got inside and the dishes were done and the floor had been vacuumed. I walked into the back yard where Nick, Jackson, and Blake were pulling weeds and saw that it had also been mowed.

"Why didn't you just tell me why you wanted me to take Alex?" I asked Nick.

"Because then it wouldn't have been a surprise," he said.

Just give me the whole dang pie.

SLEEPING ON THE COUCH

I put my scrambled eggs in a bowl just as Blake came into the kitchen and asked for a bowl of Cheerios. I got the milk out of the fridge while Nick got the cereal out of the pantry, then took the lid off of the milk and poured it on my eggs. I didn't realize my mistake until Nick looked at Blake's empty bowl, then at my milk-covered eggs and started laughing. Good old pregnancy brain!

Pregnancy teaches mothers-to-be to locate a bathroom everywhere they go, and that after a certain point their husband will have to shave their legs for them or deal with the rough reality of the consequences. It also taught me pregnancy nightmares can be quite literal. If I have a bad dream, I scream myself awake when it starts to get scary. Each time I was with child, the vivid dreams typical of pregnancy made this a regular occurrence. Unfortunately, the joke about husbands sleeping on the couch was always on me. Nick has never slept on the couch. I, however, have come to know it all too well.

While pregnant with Jackson, I slept on the couch to avoid waking Nick every time I had to barf. Expecting for the first time, I wasn't aware there were hour-by-hour pregnancy guides and check-off lists to follow. But if by "do yoga," they meant get on your hands and knees and pray to the porcelain god, I had it covered. Pull over and fling the car door open to throw up on the side of the road . . . check! Go out to eat then get home and flush the money I spent on dinner straight down the toilet . . . check!

With Blake, I had insomnia. I lay on that same hand-me-down couch I slept on when I was pregnant with Jackson and surfed two hundred channels of infomercials. On the bright side, I am now prepared to be a ShamWow demonstrator in my next life. Perhaps I'll introduce a line of ultra-absorbent, ShamWow-lined diapers.

Being pregnant with Aaron gave me debilitating back pain, so I slept on the couch for extra back support. By then, I had acquired the complete series of *Gilmore Girls* on DVD, so at least I was well entertained by witty one-liners. If I ever hear anyone complain about how there's nothing to watch on Netflix, I'll give them the old speech about how I had to walk barefoot in the snow, uphill both ways, to find a Blockbuster Video Store so I could rent *Adventures in Babysitting*.

Also during that pregnancy, my relationship with the couch took an interesting twist when Aaron turned himself into breech position two weeks before his due date. The doctor tried to turn him but he wouldn't budge. I really didn't want a c-section, so I tried all kinds of stuff trying to get him to flip back into a head-down position, including propping an ironing board up against the couch and lying upside down on it. When that didn't work, I blamed it on the couch; it never liked me anyway. By the grace of God, the doctor was willing to deliver the baby breech and Aaron ended up being my easiest delivery.

When I found out I was pregnant with Alex, I was determined to own my pregnancy instead of letting it own me. And to sleep in my own bed. The first thing I had to take control of was the refried Taco Bell addiction that called my name morning, noon, and night. I could also down a bag of Lindt truffles like nobody's business, so I banned myself from buying more than a single truffle at a time. Eating whatever I wanted whenever I wanted seemed like a good idea each time a craving hit, but from experience I knew I would be cursing my overindulgence the day the baby was born. I made a serious effort to eat fruit and drink yogurt smoothies instead, and it didn't take long before I could drive past the tempting pink and purple bell without salivating. Cravings: owned.

I also enlisted a friend and went walking five days a week. I may have been as round and wobbly as a bowling ball pushed by a toddler, but I never ended up in the gutter. Sometimes a root canal sounded more appealing than exercise, but when my walking buddy knocked on the door, I had no choice but to get moving. Physical fitness: owned.

When I couldn't possibly wear my regular jeans for one more day, I pulled out the box of maternity clothes that had been banished to the garage. I stared at the wrinkly, misshapen jeans hibernating inside and wanted to go back in time and kick myself for ever buying them in the first place. Ew! And why on earth were we storing tents in the same box? Never mind, those were maternity shirts. Double ew! I headed to the mall and bought new clothes so I didn't look as unsightly as I felt and discovered skirts were the way to go. They were more comfortable than jeans, and I didn't have to pull them back up over my belly every time I bent down to load the dishwasher. Pregnancy threads: owned.

I cheated my pregnancy with Alex right up until the third trimester. I only gained fifteen pounds and managed to stave off most of the aches and pains that accompanied my previous nine-month parasite-hosting experiences. I even slept well at night, in my bed. I thought I was all that—forget the bag of chips! But alas, the grand equilibrium of Mother Nature let me know my pregnancy wasn't over yet. And that I would not emerge an uncontested victor.

One night during month seven, I woke up with a tight, chest-crushing pain Google thought was heartburn. I'd had heartburn before, and on a scale of 1 to *did you want to breathe with that?* it was off the charts. Cyberspace was full of suggestions on how to ease the pain, but I was fresh out of aloe vera juice, so I drank a glass of baking soda water and got on the dreadmill. A forty-five minute walk finally made me feel better, then I found myself lying on that blasted couch.

The heartburn returned for several consecutive nights, and the couch and I became re-acquainted; just like old times. The chest pain eventually subsided altogether and I made it back to my bed. After only a few peaceful nights, a charley horse jolted me awake. I grabbed Nick's arm and woke him from a deep sleep, scaring him half to death.

"What is it?" he sat up and asked urgently.

"My leg is cramping and I can't move," I painfully whispered.

I knew the best way to stop a charley horse was to flex my foot and press it into the floor, but between my huge belly and the intense pain, I couldn't move. Instead, Nick pushed against the bottom of my foot until my leg calmed down enough that I could stand up.

I started taking antacids before bed because the calcium was supposed to help prevent muscle cramps, but they still came. Their rude awakening always incited panic, but the remedy became routine. Without saying anything, I would grab Nick's arm in a desperate plea for help, and he'd pop up like a Jack-in-the-Box. He would press against my foot until I stopped biting my lip—a sure sign the pain was gone—and go right back to sleep. I'd be too afraid to lie back down in case I got another cramp, and I'd once again find myself on that loathsome couch.

I never hated the couch more during all my pregnancies than I did during that seventh month with Alex when a cracked tooth laid me flat for days. On a Friday afternoon, around the time when dentist offices close for the weekend, I started to feel something in one of my top teeth. It didn't actually hurt, so I figured I could live with the annoyance for the weekend and deal with it on Monday morning. By bedtime, it hurt bad. Ibuprofen is banned during pregnancy, so I took some acetaminophen, but it was about as effective in providing relief as a piece of gum would have been.

The pain in my tooth got progressively worse until I made a trip to the ER late Saturday night, begging for some pregnancy-approved pain killers. The doctor gave me the best thing he could, but all the good stuff was off limits. I spent the rest of the weekend with a hot, rice-filled sock pressed against my cheek, watching cheesy *find my single friend/widowed parent a spouse for Christmas* movies on the couch.

Monday morning, the dentist took one look at my x-ray and told me my tooth had to go. It was a crowned tooth I had a root canal on fifteen years earlier, which killed the nerve. For that reason, I didn't feel anything until the infection inside the crown spread far enough that it hit my sinuses. The best solution was to pull the tooth and get an implant, which usually merits sedation. But in my delicate state, I could only have local anesthetic and sub-par pain pills after the fact. It was going to be a rocky road (mmm…rocky road!). When the dentist told me how much an implant was going to cost, my pregnancy hormones took over and I started crying.

"Tell me what you're nervous about," he said.

"I'm just pregnant," I replied, and he laughed out loud. I couldn't have expected anything less; it's hard enough for men to handle their own wives when tears start to flow, let alone a pregnant stranger. Another week of sleeping on the couch and a few thousand rounds of Candy Crush later, I was finally back in my bed.

———

I thought the couch was my least favorite place to sleep until I was in a hospital bed waiting for Alex to arrive; then I remembered I hated hospital beds even more. Lying uncomfortably in a cold room trying to find something on TV to distract me from excruciating contractions while people poke me with needles is definitely worse. The anesthetist who gave me an epidural was supposed to make me more comfortable by blocking the pain, which would have also made everything else less annoying, but he did nothing of the sort.

Epidurals should only be administered by women who have given birth. If that had been the case, maybe the anesthetist would have listened to me. When the needle was going in, I told him it hurt but he didn't seem to care about how this was my fourth epidural and I knew it shouldn't make me feel like I wanted to turn around and punch him in the face. He kept pushing, so I screamed, and when he didn't stop, I screamed at him. "Dude! Seriously! Ow!" He pushed just a little more and I screamed even louder. "STOP! I know this isn't supposed to feel like this!" He finally took it out and tried again. Thankfully, the second try only hurt a normal amount.

Regardless of that unpleasant episode, the anesthetist still thought he knew better than I did when I told him the medicine wasn't strong enough. He supposedly amped it up, but I didn't feel a difference. During childbirth, the Silent Speech Giver is anything but silent. "Sir, when I spend over a thousand dollars not to feel pain, I should be feeling a lot less than I am," I said with a major side of sass. Then I realized I should probably be nice to the person giving me pain killers, even if he did hurt me. My tone did a 180 and I said, "Please make the medicine a lot stronger. It doesn't feel like it's working at all."

Whether he actually increased the dosage or I had already incurred his wrath and he only pretended to, I'll never know. But I do know I felt everything I never wanted to, and along with my precious new baby, I got to take home a nasty, deep purple bruise where the needle was inserted into my back. The money I spent on that unsuccessful epidural could have bought us a new couch; or at least paid for enough diapers to last until Alex is potty trained.

Babies come home with some kind of reverse potty training that makes them go to the bathroom on their parents, on their parents' beds, on the carpet, and all over their clothes. If you're changing boys you have to be fast, like lightning, or you'll get soaked. When Alex was only a few days old, I laid him on my bed to change his diaper. The second he was uncovered, a yellow stream of perfectly arced pee hit him in the face, then shot up over his head and hosed my sheets and pillowcase. He wasn't a fan of being naked (yet), and he was due for a feeding. The combination of being naked and hungry, along with the surprise that showered his face, had him screaming his guts out.

I cleaned Alex up as fast as I could and headed to the rocking chair to feed him; my sheets would have to wait. By the time he was sufficiently satiated and sleeping soundly, the sheets were dry. I was too tired to care that my baby marked his territory on them and lay down anyway. No way was I going to sleep on the couch again over that! My pillowcase was still damp, so I flipped it over and went to sleep. Nick was downstairs when it happened, and since his pillowcase didn't get sprayed, I figured what he didn't know wouldn't hurt him. Desperate times call for selfish measures.

During those January nights when Alex was new enough that I could still see heaven in his eyes, his hungry cries landed us both on the couch. This time, though, Alex and I got to share quiet moments in the firelight as he wrapped his tiny fingers around mine and ate. When he fell back to sleep, I'd wrap him in a soft, warm blanket and lay him on against the back of the couch. Then I'd pull our big LoveSac up next to it and take a nap until he was ready to eat again. Watching Alex's sleeping eyes flutter as he slowly released his binky, continuing to suck right up until it fell out of his mouth, changed the way I felt about the couch. With each peaceful breath Alex took, the couch where his tiny head rested finally redeemed itself.

FAMILY PHOTO SESSION

It's so funny how you can see yourself in the mirror every day and then look at a picture and think, "Do I really look like that?"

I like to get pictures taken of my kids, and my husband, and my husband with my kids. But I'm always waiting to lose twenty pounds before I'll be ready to let the camera capture my unforgiving curves. When I realize how few pictures we have with me in them, and that I'm not getting any younger, I know it's time for a family photo session—whether I like it or not.

Once a date is set, there's a long list of choices to be made. Bad decisions will be documented in living color for generations to come, so it's not a matter to be taken lightly. I certainly don't want to pay good money for a picture that should be Facebook cover photo worthy and still not be able to replace the one from three Christmases ago, which is missing my youngest child. It's worth losing a little sleep over to get it right, for social media's sake!

First, we have to decide on a location. Location, location, location! I Google every barn, field, and body of water within a thirty mile radius to find the one that will make my family look the most angelic. An old bridge is even better, and if I happen to find a bridge over a stream with a barn in the distance, I should probably buy a lottery ticket because I've struck gold!

Next, I undertake the daunting task of figuring out what everyone will wear. I search Pinterest for coordinating color palettes and learn I need to mix patterns and solids for more dynamic photos. Then I raid every closet and dresser drawer and look under every bed to see what we already have that fits into the color scheme. If I'm going to stick with my chosen colors, I'm limited to a Thomas the Train T-shirt and Star Wars pajamas. The kids can either wear the same shirts they wore for their last set of pictures, or I get to go shopping!

After flipping through every hanger in my closet twice and lamenting the fact that the only clothes I want to wear are still waiting for me to fit into them again (I blame it on the baby, it couldn't possibly be my chocolate-covered almond addiction), I make a change of plans. This photo shoot will be for the kids. I'd rather look at pictures of myself from when I was twenty-three anyway. I'd give anything to have that body back (anything besides sugar and time at the gym, apparently). I tell Nick I'm bowing out, and he immediately vetoes my decision because taking family pictures was my idea to begin with. So, I'm back to square one: what am *I* going to wear?

Before I head to the mall, I take a shoe inventory. Everyone's shoes will need to be photogenic enough for a family shoe shot, and they will need to match each other. I don't want any lasting evidence that my kid walks around with a huge hole in the toe of his right shoe because Spider-Man is the only character worthy to go on his feet. Getting him to wear nice shoes for a few hours may require a serious ice cream sundae, but I do what I have to do.

When the big day arrives, I pour myself a large glass of patience, which I'll need in order to fight the resistance. Shoes will be too tight, tags too itchy, and belts too belty. Shirt collars will bug, brothers will bug, and actual bugs will bug. Whose idea was it to have an outside photo shoot again?

In the car, I try to explain the difference between a natural smile and a fake smile to the kids. Jackson has a harder time with this than anyone. He smiles on command, but it often looks forced and, quite frankly, can be a little creepy. Blake's dimpled smile looks natural enough, but he does an automatic head tilt with every snap as if he's mistaking the family photo session for an old-school V8 commercial.

Aaron wants a collage of himself making silly faces and has figured out how to play the photographer. He smiles right up until she steps behind the camera, then sticks out his tongue, rolls his eyes, pulls at the corners of his mouth, and shoots Spider-Man webs. We even have a photo of him looking right at the camera and unintentionally giving it his middle finger. Nice.

Alex isn't going to be happy no matter what, so he'll either be crying or sucking on his binky in every picture. Or, there is that split second—right after Mom yanks the binky but just before he realizes it's gone—that results in a classic open-mouth, deer-in-the-headlights look.

When it's time for the kids' individual pictures, I get my crazy on and do funny things to make them laugh. This seems to have more potential to make their smiles big and genuine than a drawn out "cheese" does. My tactics may include, but are certainly not limited to, playing peek-a-boo, jumping around like a monkey, making silly faces, and pretending to swat an imaginary mosquito on the top of my head. This approach usually yields favorable results, but it can also backfire if instead of laughing, the kids stare at me like I've fallen off the cuckoo wagon.

We make it through the session and breathe a sigh of relief that it's over (this time anyway), then anxiously await the digital results. When the pictures are ready, I look through them with the fresh memory of the effort we put into getting everyone to look up and look happy at the same time. In almost every shot, one child is either blinking, blankly staring, or simply not smiling. I wonder why the photographer has a magazine coveresque photo of every family featured on their website, yet ours isn't fooling anyone. But hey, at least our shoes matched!

After some time passes and I look at the pictures again, I realize the best ones capture the way we really are, and I'm glad we have them. Expecting the unexpected is a general rule for a family photo session, but the last time we had our pictures taken, I was hit with something I could have never prepared for. As I stood behind the photographer, who was taking a picture of Nick with the boys, I looked at Alex and realized I would never have a baby that small again. My eyes started to well up, and the emotion caught me completely off guard because I was the first to say he would be our last.

Sometimes I daydream about the day when all my kids are in school so I can go to the gym, or out to lunch without having to either find a babysitter or make a futile attempt to keep the little one happy in a restaurant high chair. I imagine being able to sit at the computer and write for hours at a time without having to make PBJs, break up fights, or block chubby little fingers from attacking the keyboard. So maybe I was just sad that if my kids were getting older, I was too. I doubt it though, because when I thought about all the slobbery kisses I needed to soak up and all the adorably unsteady first steps I needed to archive before they were nothing more than memories, I felt a tug on my heartstrings. My unexpected avalanche of nostalgia helped me realize first words and deep-belly baby laughs far outweigh the lost sleep that comes from a nursing or teething baby, and I wished I could bottle them up and keep them forever.

Even with all the location hunting, pattern coordinating, and smile coaching, there are some things no photographer will ever be able capture. Like the proud feeling I got when Jackson's teacher told me he hadn't missed a single spelling word all year, or the way Blake tells stories that go on, and on, and on. If there was a picture of the fear in their eyes when Aaron manhandled his brothers to the ground, it would perfectly sum up what life was like when he was two. And no printed picture could possibly describe the bittersweet feelings that came when we gave away the baby clothes Alex grew out of, especially since many of them had been worn by all four of my babies. Whether recorded in writing or in a special place in the heart, preserving those memories is the job of the mamarazzi.

HEELS AND CHURCH DON'T MIX

Church starts at 11:00 am. At 10:53, Nick sent Blake to ask me if I was ready.

Blake: *Mom, Dad wants to know if you're ready to go.*

Me: *Yes, tell him to go ahead and get you guys in the car.*

Blake left and as he was walking downstairs, I heard him say, "She'll be like eleven minutes."

He's onto me!

———

No matter how early I get out of bed to start getting ready, we are late to church ninety percent of the time. It doesn't help that Nick often has to be to the church early for meetings, so I'm frequently helping the kids get ready on my own. Going to church isn't like running a quick errand where there's only a slim chance I'll see someone I know. At church, I know everyone I see. Not only do I have to look presentable, but I also have to avoid the cardinal sin of wearing the same thing two weeks in a row. The problem is I don't always remember what I wore to church the previous week. Nick says if I can't remember, neither will anyone else. But his logic is flawed; if I'm wearing the same dress I wore the last time my church friends saw me, they'll remember.

When I finally arrive with the kids, we parade ourselves down the aisle to where Nick is saving us a seat, followed by the eyes of everyone who got to 11:00 church on time. The kids squabble about who gets to sit by Dad because he usually has LifeSavers in his pocket. Even though everyone always gets one, the kids' proximity to the sugar seems to calm the fear that they might miss out. Once everyone is settled, the kids unzip their coats, which sounds ten times louder at church than anywhere else, and stuff them under the bench. You definitely can't miss us, or the outfit I'm wearing.

If Aaron pursues a career as an escape artist, it will be a direct result of the schemes his two-year-old mind conjured up to pull off successful church breakouts. At that age, his talent for breaking free was exceptional. One week in the middle of the service, Aaron saw a woman open the large double doors leading from the chapel out into the hallway and tore out of there like the DeLorean time machine on its way back to the future. His momentum gave him enough strength to push open the glass door leading outside, and by the time I caught up to him he was one step away from running into the parking lot.

Nick and I tried to block Aaron in by sitting on opposite ends of the bench, but where there's an iron-willed two-year-old, there's a way. After growing bored with unsuccessfully trying to climb over Nick's leg, Aaron dropped to the floor, crawled under the bench, popped up in front of the people sitting behind us, and took off.

I stopped wearing high heels to church once I had kids. Holding a baby and/or chasing a toddler in shoes requiring me to either walk gracefully or eat dirt just didn't seem safe. Aaron was almost three the first time I dared to wear heels to church again. That was my first mistake. Halfway through the service, Nick went up to the front of the chapel to sing with the choir. Not moving to the aisle seat Nick vacated, which left nothing between Aaron and freedom, was my second mistake. When Aaron started to get squirmy, I leaned over Jackson's lap and whispered, "Look Aaron, Daddy's up there singing." That was my third mistake.

Aaron saw Nick and raced toward him. By the time I stepped over Jackson and leaned forward to grab Aaron, he was just out of reach. I could have taken my heels off and sprinted, but we were in church, so I decided against it. I didn't gain much ground before Aaron was up on the stand pulling at the skirts and slacks of other choir members in search of his Dad. When Aaron finally found the right pair of pants to tug on—the ones with LifeSavers in the pockets— Nick picked him up and held him for the remainder of the performance. I haven't worn heels to church since.

Once when I was waiting for my kids to get out of their primary classes (where they learn about God the Father, Jesus Christ, and things like honesty and serving others), a woman I had seen regularly but had never before talked to came up to me and said, "I don't mean to insult you . . ." I braced myself for the unsolicited advice she was about to give on how to keep my kids quiet during church and wrestled the Silent Speech Giver into submission. The woman continued, "My niece has two boys who are a little older than your kids and asked me if I know anyone who might like the clothes they've grown out of. I wondered if you could use them." How quickly I assumed she was going to reprimand me when she was actually extending a kindness; talk about paranoid!

That same sweet lady followed me out of the chapel and into the hallway one Sunday when Nick wasn't there, offering to bounce a tired and crying Baby Alex so I could go back in with the three kids I left sitting alone. On my way out, I passed them some Smarties and told them to behave while I tried to get Alex to sleep. Good idea Mom: load them up with sugar, leave them, and expect them to sit quietly. Sometimes, I'm a special kind of scatterbrained.

When I'm in the hallway with a little one (or two) instead of listening to the church service, or when I can't pay attention because someone is climbing on my lap or over the back of the bench we're sitting on, I wonder if there's a point to taking my kids to church. But then I hear Jackson pray and ask Heavenly Father to help him fall asleep quickly, which has always been a challenge for him, or listen to Aaron pray that his cough will go away so he doesn't have to miss preschool again, and I know it's worth the fight.

My kids know they have a Father in Heaven who loves them and who cares about what they have to say. They know if they have a problem, they can pray about how to solve it, and that they will get an answer. At church, they also learn what the Holy Spirit feels like so when their answers do come, they can recognize them. I want them to learn to talk to Heavenly Father as soon as they can say, "Dada," because He is the only perfect parent, and His advice is infinitely better than mine.

RAW, ORGANIC MOM GUILT

Aaron: Mom, Alex has your issues.

I ruined him already, huh? We didn't even make it a year.

Me: What issues?

Aaron: The ones you eat.

I looked over and saw Alex shaking a can of cashews. Issues . . . cashews . . . whatever!

———

The first gift motherhood gave me was guilt: 100% raw, organic mom guilt. It is a no-holds-barred emotion that digs deep, wrapping its nagging claws around a woman's soul and holding on for dear life.

I ate too much sugar while I was pregnant, which is the

reason my son loves candy (yeah, that's it). I didn't play enough classical music while he was in the womb, which severely reduced his potential for musical talent. I didn't put locking latches on the cabinets before I went into labor. Now my baby, who won't even be able to roll over for three months, or crawl for six, has access to the dish soap under the sink. What kind of person doesn't baby proof their house before bringing a baby into it?

I've had all types of different work situations since having children, and mom guilt has tormented me in every single one of them. When I worked full-time in an office, I felt guilty I wasn't able to nurse my baby at every feeding. When I worked from home with my kids running wild, I was constantly pushing them away and saying, "Later honey, I have to get this done right now." Later often turned into tomorrow, which turned into tears over broken promises at bedtime, and the claws of guilt sank in deeper. When I worked from home and the kids went to day care, I felt guilty because they knew I was home and sent them off anyway. When I became a stay at home—without also having to work from home—mom, I thought the guilt would go away. I should have known better; there's still plenty of guilt to go around.

I feel guilty when Nick comes home to a house that looks like it was hit by a tornado (two of them, actually, named Aaron and Alex). I'm sorry I didn't sweep up after their most recent snack and pick up all the toys they carted around, because a cluttered house doesn't offer a very warm welcome. But if I tried to keep up with their messes, I would never do anything else.

Guilt over a messy house, however, is nothing compared to the guilt I feel for not loving every second of being home with my kids, no matter how much I love them. Catering to little people who constantly need to be fed, calmed, changed, wiped, held, and played with can be exhausting. When I complain about it, sometimes Nick reminds me it's what I wanted. Even though he's right, it never goes over well. The Silent Speech Giver has her response down pat.

I wanted to stop feeling like I wasn't giving enough time to our family, not to feel like all I'm good for is to be a snot rag and a sounding board for whining, crying, fighting children. At least you get to leave the house and feel like you've accomplished something every day. I would love to go out of town every couple of weeks and sleep in a silent hotel room.

I don't let her say it, because there's no use in trying to make Nick feel guilty just because I'm a drama-fest. Nick works hard to support our family and supports me in whatever I choose to do, but I will never be good enough for myself, and there's nothing he can do about that. I wish my emotional strength was as solid as the death grip of a toddler who doesn't want to be left with a babysitter, but I can't even argue with a four-year-old without sinking to his level.

One day, when I'm arguing with teenagers over curfews and car keys, I'm sure I'll look back on the days when our disagreements were over wearing coats and eating vegetables as if they were a dream. I try to remember this each time Aaron wants to play Spot it! for hours on end, but I swear I have chronic cabin fever. And yes, I feel guilty about that too.

———

When I was pregnant with Alex, Nick's job took him out of town more than usual. I was therefore left alone to manage the mayhem on a more regular basis, and to lie awake wondering if the sounds I heard in the middle of the night were escaped prisoners. I wanted some "me time" before Alex arrived and the prospect of taking a childless vacation got pushed out a few more years, so I told Nick I needed to get away for a few days. "What are you waiting for?" he asked. I wasn't waiting anymore.

I called my friend Jenette and asked her if she wanted to go on vacation with a prego lady. I warned her that it would basically be liked traveling with a child since I would need a lot of snacks and would have to go to the bathroom all the time, and she still said yes. We consulted our calendars and booked flights to Washington, D.C. Sweet mercy, five whole days without having to make dinner! Let freedom ring! The first thing I wanted to see was the Declaration of Independence. Coincidence? I think not!

When I called home on the second day of our trip, Nick told me the kids were all sick. Blake had been up most of the night coughing, Jackson was lying on the floor and didn't want to move, and Aaron had a fever. Even though my husband was perfectly capable, I felt terrible they were all feeling miserable and I wasn't there to help them. I ran clear to the other side of the country and mom guilt still found me, reminding me I could run, but I could never hide.

Although I felt bad being away from my little sickies,

the trip was a great time for me to do some soul-searching. Jenette earned a master's degree from George Washington University in D.C., and still had friends living in the area. We visited her friend Liz, who worked at a Smithsonian Museum on the National Mall. She and Jenette talked about their museum jobs, and I had nothing to contribute to the conversation. I started thinking about the monuments we planned to see the following day, and couldn't recall nearly as much about the men they stand as a tribute to as I should have been able to.

Who wrote the Federalist Papers? John Adams? I checked my smart phone and boy, did it make me feel dumb. The Federalist Papers were written by three different men, and Adams was not one of them. At that point, the Silent Speech Giver turned on me and instead of defending me like she usually does, she made me feel worse. *What do you have to say for yourself now, history major? Stop pretending you're smart. That girl is long gone.*

After that, I stopped digging around for buried knowledge, because it just made me want to dig myself a hole to crawl into. But I did know all the words to the Teenage Mutant Ninja Turtles theme song, does that count for anything?

I returned my attention to the girls' conversation and wondered if I would have been good at working in a museum before my brain turned to mush. I probably would have. Right then, fireworks went off in my head and I had a grand epiphany as to what my problem really was. I don't love staying home with my kids because I don't feel like I'm good at it.

The world of sports-loving, energetic boys is the polar opposite of the world I lived in before I had boys of my own. I was never good at sports, so I never played them. At least, not voluntarily. The one time I agreed to play volleyball without a grade hinging on my participation was only because the boy who invited me to the pool party was incredibly good looking (he never asked me out again). I've never handled chaos very well either. I used to hide from my rowdy brothers by getting cozy on my bed and reading everything from John Grisham novels to my Art History book.

Once I realized my biggest problem is I don't feel like I'm good at raising boys, I pondered it on a deeper level and figured out my biggest fear. My biggest fear is I'm ruining my rambunctious little men with my impatience. No wonder I don't shed glitter and radiate sunshine: I'm always living in guilt and fear. Although I hadn't been able to add much to Liz and Jenette's conversation, the one I had with myself was highly educational.

On the last day of our trip, Jenette and I visited Arlington National Cemetery. There, we saw the Changing of the Guard at the Tomb of the Unknown Soldier. Spectators watching the ceremony sit on steps directly across from the Tomb, where silence is mandatory and no food is allowed.

Two steps below us sat a mom with dark, naturally curly hair who was surrounded by three little boys. Her kids looked slightly younger than the three I had left at home, and I silently applauded her bravery. The youngest boy, who was about eighteen months old, started to get restless before the ceremony started. His mom carried him over to where his stroller was parked and gave him a snack. She could see her other kids the whole time, but couldn't talk to them without breaking the reverent silence. I watched in amazement as the two brothers sat perfectly still until their mom returned. Every once in a while, they looked in her direction, but neither of them said a word. The ceremony started just after she sat back down, and the boys watched respectfully until the end.

Once we left the no talking zone, I walked over to the woman and said, "I also have three boys and I want to tell you that your kids were amazing during that, especially when you took the little one away and left the other two alone. I can't believe how quietly they sat."

A visible wave of relief washed over her face. Sadly, she probably thought I was going to criticize her or offer unsolicited advice on how her children should have acted, even though they were angels. She smiled and said, "Thank you. It's so nice to hear that you're doing something right. It doesn't always feel that way."

"I know, boys are hard to keep quiet, but they were awesome," I said. She proudly smiled at her kids and thanked me again. I was kind-of nervous to talk to her, simply because she was a stranger. But after spending a few days thinking about how I never felt like I was good at being a mother, I wanted to give her some encouragement.

I'm glad I ignored my nerves long enough to talk to her, because she validated my feelings without knowing it. There she was, a beautiful mother of three well-behaved children making the effort to show them something special, saying she didn't always feel like she was doing it right. Insanity, thy name is guilt!

———

I didn't see Jenette again for almost a year because we live in different states. When I finally did, we were chatting over breakfast at Corner Bakery Café and she asked me how things were going.

"Fine," I said. "But I haven't really done anything since I saw you last, so I don't have much to tell."

"Are you kidding me Amber?" she said and looked at me like I misunderstood the question. I thought back to sweeping the kitchen floor a million times, standing next to my bed folding laundry, picking kids up from school, and trying to keep them from killing each other. Nope, nothing noteworthy. I looked back at her and shrugged my shoulders.

"Except that you gave birth and have been raising four kids every single day. How is that nothing?" When she opened that door, I took the opportunity to throw a bunch of emotional baggage right through it.

"Well yeah, but I don't do it very well. And half the time, I'm a disaster. I wish I could learn to think with my brain instead of my emotions and be happy with what I have."

She laughed. "Well, if you figure out how, let me know, because I also have that problem."

"My kids are just kids," I continued. "They don't deserve to have a mom who gets annoyed just because they're loud.

It's not like they're doing anything wrong, that's what kids are: loud. I look at them and think, 'I'm sorry this is what you get for a mom.' And I feel bad for them."

Jenette shook her head and said, "Your kids are lucky to have you. They're lucky to have someone who loves them, and who tries her best even if she's not perfect. Everyone wishes they were better at something. I'm sure my mom wishes she had done some things differently, but I know she loves me, and always has. And I love her for trying. Your kids know you love them, and that's important."

I do love my kids, but I thought back to all the times I didn't show it very well. I should have let Jackson stay up an extra twenty minutes so we could play checkers together; it would have been worth it. I shouldn't have gotten mad at Blake when he pushed Aaron down; after all, Aaron started it. And I definitely shouldn't have freaked out when Aaron broke the oven door off of the play kitchen in the toy room. The kids could still play with the rest of it, and one day it will end up at the dump. But my regret will live on.

By the look on my face, Jenette could tell I wasn't sold. "Listen to me," she said and looked me in the eye. "Your kids are lucky to have you."

I hoped one day I would feel the same way.

SILVER LININGS

This is what summer sounds like to me: What are we going to do today? That again? Why can't we do something else? He's hurting me. He already used his screen time and he's still playing. I need a snack. It's my turn. I need a drink. He's bugging me. And an occasional, "Thanks Mom."

But when Jackson told me summer was "better than awesome," I knew I did something right!

———

A common plea from me to my kids sounds something like, "Dudes, I'm tired of you fighting and hurting each other, can you please play nicely together while I finish making dinner?" They always promise to calm down, then run away tripping each other and trying to elbow one another out of the way. So much for that!

However, there are times when my kids do things that let me know their ears do work. Even if they are concentrating on making the hole in their sock bigger while I'm talking to them, it's encouraging to know they are (occasionally) listening.

The year Jackson went into second grade and Blake started kindergarten, Nick and I talked to them about including and being nice to everyone. We acted out scenarios where we were mean to each other and had the kids practice what they should do and say in different situations.

"Can I play soccer with you at recess?" I asked Nick.

"No, you're not good enough to be on my team," he said. I frowned and pretended to cry and the kids laughed. Then one of them took Nick's place and I asked if I could be on their team at recess. They simply said, "Sure," and laughed some more. They thought it was silly, but we wanted them to know what to do when our pretend situations presented themselves in reality.

Blake got an opportunity to be a friend to someone in need on his very first day of school. A girl in his class broke her leg over the summer and had to be in a wheelchair for six weeks. She was sitting alone at recess watching the other kids play, so Blake sat by her and they made up a game to play. He told me they were going to play it again the next day, and I wanted to bear hug him and put a glittery gold star on his forehead.

Jackson was also in a situation early in the year where he had to choose whether he was going to include someone who was being deliberately excluded or not. He was playing with some kids at recess who told another boy he couldn't join them, so Jackson told the kids to let the boy play too. They decided Jackson couldn't play with them anymore either, so he and the other boy played together instead. Luckily in boy world, most playground spats end when recess does. The next day, all the boys played together, including the one who was left out in the first place.

It was therefore befitting when I found a Valentine Jackson made sitting out on the table (so of course I had to read it!), giving instructions on how to be a friend. He had traced his hand onto a piece of paper and in the middle of the hand, it said, "How to be a friend." On each finger, he wrote the instructions. *1) Be nice. 2) Be a good person. 3) Be helpful to one another. 4) Feel good for what you have and not for what other people have. 5) Be courageous if someone is bullying one of your friends and tell them to stop.* Sometimes, through a child's eyes is the best way to approach life.

Aaron, our little ball of atomic energy, has also had times where he's slowed down long enough to think of others. When he was two and couldn't say many words, we were eating lunch at someone else's house and one of their friends stopped by. Aaron still had half of a grilled cheese sandwich on his plate when he reached for the platter in the middle of the table to take another. I told him to first finish what he had, so he took one bite and then reached for the platter again. After several rounds of that, I finally let him get a new sandwich. With the uneaten sandwich in hand, he climbed down from his chair and handed it to the man who had stopped by. I'm glad I finally gave in so he could show me he was learning to share.

When Aaron was four, he momentarily melted my heart in the bread aisle at Costco. He was sitting cross-legged in the cart poking at the tops of poppy seed muffins when he randomly looked up at me and said, "You're my love."

"And you're my love," I said back.

A woman who was there with her daughter looked over and smiled at us. For about five seconds, I was overjoyed to be the object of Aaron's affection. And if he ever tried to deny it, I had a witness. Then he hit me with, "No Mom, not you. They say it on a movie."

"Well, you're still my love," I said and heard the other woman laugh the kind of laugh that spits itself out when you're trying to suppress it. It was nice while it lasted, anyway.

The best way to know kids understand something you're trying to teach them is when they're able to teach it to someone else, not only with words but through their actions. On Christmas Eve, we went to a party where Santa made an appearance at 7:30 pm. It was the third time my kids had seen him, and the first two times Blake had asked for a Lego set. That night, he asked for Mario Party 9 for the Wii instead, which he had never before played or mentioned. Amazon is still researching their thirty-minute drone delivery system, so there was no possible way for me to make it happen.

That same year, Jackson asked for a watch featuring his favorite MLS soccer team, which he wanted more than anything else on his list. (Here's a tip: when Christmas shopping online, use an incognito window. Otherwise things you look at will show up in Google ads and your kids' lists will get longer.)

We wanted to save the best for last, so we wrapped the watch and set it inside the Christmas tree branches. In the midst of twinkling lights and the glittery snowflake ornaments that reflected off of them, the gift was well hidden.

When all the presents under the tree had been opened and Mario Party 9 was nowhere to be found, Blake said, "Santa didn't bring me what I asked for." I explained to him that he had seen Santa three times and asked for a Lego set the first two, which he did get. But when he changed his request on Christmas Eve and Santa was already out delivering presents, it was too late.

Then Jackson helped out by saying, "But Blake, look at all your cool stuff. I love everything I got," without mentioning the watch.

"Jackson, what's that?" Nick asked, pointing to the box in the tree. Jackson didn't see anything at first, but walked over to the tree and pulled it out. When he unwrapped his new watch, the huge grin on his face screamed, "Thanks a million!" The bigger thanks, though, was that he was grateful for what he had, even before he got what he wanted most.

———

At the end of the day, even if I'm disappointed in my parental shortcomings, one thing I know is my kids will have each other's backs. A perfect example of this was a generous offer Jackson made to Blake. Blake likes watermelon, but not watermelon seeds; not even the white ones. Before he'll touch it, I have to cut it into small cubes and pick the seeds out with a fork. One summer afternoon, Jackson saw a watermelon in the fridge and asked Blake if he wanted some. Blake thought about it and said no. "I'll take all the seeds out for you," Jackson offered. No matter how old you are, there's always something nice you can do for someone else!

The day before Christmas break, the student council at Jackson and Blake's school delivered candygrams the students had purchased for their friends. I hadn't heard anything about it until Blake brought one home, signed by Jackson, who took his own money to school to buy it for him. Raiding the piggy bank you've been slowly filling to buy a new videogame is a sure sign of brotherly love!

Blake also worries about his brothers. When Jackson was in kindergarten, he usually left for school before Blake woke up. One morning at 6:50, Blake came running into our bedroom with Jackson's backpack strapped on his shoulders. "Dad!" he exclaimed, waking us both up. "Jackson forgot his backpack! See? It's still here," he said. The look of urgency on his face would have probably been the same if the house was on fire.

"He's still asleep, it's not time to get up yet," Nick told him. That wasn't enough reassurance for Blake, so he opened Jackson's door to make sure he was in his bed. He smiled and said, "Oh," then went back to sleep.

In Blake's kindergarten class, there was a treasure box the kids got to choose a prize from when they did exceptionally well, helped the teacher, or achieved an accomplishment. When Blake got to choose a prize for returning a note the teacher needed back ASAP, he saw a Goofy figurine he knew Aaron would like and chose it instead of taking something for himself. Aaron was so excited that Blake brought something home for him that he swiped a Starburst from my purse to give Blake in return. I'm not usually a fan of the kids swiping my emergency stash because it serves me well when a child has a meltdown in the grocery store or is all of a sudden starving. But that day, I let it slide.

When Baby Alex joined our family, Aaron took to him like he was a long-lost friend and always made sure he was taken care of. I took the two of them on a long, ten-hour road trip to see my grandpa when he was dangerously ill, just in case it was the last time. When Alex was tired of being in his car seat, Aaron sang to him, shook his rattle, gave him graham crackers, and made silly faces to make him laugh. Aaron also patiently played Alex's favorite game a million times over, which was to throw his sippy cup in Aaron's direction, then wait for Aaron to give it back so he could throw it again.

Aaron doesn't trust anyone else to properly care for his baby brother, not even me. "Make sure he's warm enough Mom," he'll tell me before I put Alex to bed. Or, "Don't forget to feed Alex Mom, in case he be's hungry in the car." One of my favorite things he did was set up a huge barrier of chairs and bar stools so Alex couldn't get to the cabinet under the sink after the safety latch broke. Alex is in good hands, even if those hands occasionally take away things he really wants, like Cheerios that have been swept into a dirt pile on the kitchen floor. After Alex was born, Aaron earned himself the name, "Carin' Aaron."

In telling my kids what, when, and how to do things, sometimes I'm just getting in the way. I need to keep my mouth shut and my eyes open more often, because there's a lot to learn from the way my kids take care of each other. The glowing silver lining around family life is that it's a group effort, not a one-woman show.

I also greatly appreciate it when Nick and the kids make a special effort to show this woman she is loved; it's always nice to be noticed. Last Christmas, Jackson told me he knew I would like the gift he bought me because it was something I really needed. He wrapped it himself and what I opened on Christmas morning was an electronic key finder. There are plenty of times when we're already late getting out the door due to a lost shoe or last-second potty run and I can't find my keys anywhere, so I could see where he was coming from. But, I'm not sure that's quite what I'm going for when I say it's nice to be noticed. Luckily, while my kids are learning how to give gifts and show love, they have Nick for an example.

One afternoon when I wasn't feeling well, Nick called to see if there was anything I needed before he came home from work. "All I want to do is eat junk and go to bed," I said. "But don't buy me any because it will make me feel worse. Just come home." Nick had a better idea and came home with a new book for me to read. Then he sent me upstairs to rest while he made dinner and put the kids to bed. In my book, that takes the gold.

EVEN JESUS NEEDED A MOTHER

That dismal December night when Alex used my hair as leverage to pull himself into a standing position and I left Nick alone with the ball-kicking, growling kids while I went for a drive, I passed a yard featuring a life-sized nativity set. I pulled over to take a better look while I sat and enjoyed the greatest sound on earth—dead silence. In that quiet moment, a soft voice whispered, "Even Jesus needed a mother."

My mind wandered to a place and time long, long ago when Mary gave birth to the baby Jesus, far from home and under the most uncomfortable of circumstances. Jesus Christ, who had in Him the power to withstand death[2], still needed a mother to give him a body, keep him safe, and nurture Him. Not long after Jesus' birth, Mary and her husband Joseph walked to Egypt to keep the Christ Child safe from <u>King Herod</u>, who wanted him dead. Even for Mary, who was

2. James E. Talmage, *Jesus the Christ* (Salt Lake City: Deseret Book 1983), 21.

chosen by God Himself to bring the Savior and Redeemer of all mankind into the world, life was not easy.

In the 2nd chapter of Luke, The Bible tells of Jesus accompanying Mary and Joseph to Jerusalem for the feast of the Passover. Assuming Jesus was somewhere in their traveling party, Mary and Joseph completed an entire day's journey toward home before realizing he was not with them. This story reminds me of the time we lost three-year-old Jackson at a parade in Portland and helps me understand that not even Mary was a perfect mother. But because she was willing to do what God asked her to do and bring Jesus Christ into the world, He was able to carry out the atonement and fulfill his role as our Savior.

When Jesus suffered for our sins, He also suffered for our sorrows. The atonement made it possible for us to overcome sin through repentance, but also made it possible for Christ to understand our heartaches, fears, and guilt. We do have to do our best, which is sometimes better than others, but God knows we will never be perfect. For our sakes, He sent His Son to make up the difference. Thankfully, the atonement covers motherhood. And if my best is enough for God, I have to let it be good enough for me.

www.ingramcontent.com/pod-product-compliance
Lightning Source LLC
Chambersburg PA
CBHW060505030426
42337CB00015B/1750